Negotiate to succeed

Edited by Julie Lewthwaite

Viva Books

New Delhi | Mumbai | Chennai | Kolkata | Bangalore | Hyderabad | Kochi

First Indian Edition 2003
Reprinted 2008

VIVA BOOKS PRIVATE LIMITED

- 4737/23 Ansari Road, Daryaganj, New Delhi 110 002
  E-mail: vivadelhi@vivagroupindia.net, Tel. 42242200
- Plot No. 76, Service Industries, Shirvane, Sector 1, Nerul, Navi Mumbai 400 706
  E-mail: vivamumbai@vivagroupindia.net, Tel. 27721273, 27721274
- Jamals Fazal Chambers, 26 Greams Road, Chennai 600 006
  E-mail: vivachennai@vivagroupindia.net, Tel. 28290304, 28294241
- B-103, Jindal Towers, 21/1A/3 Darga Road, Kolkata 700 017
  E-mail: vivakolkata@vivagroupindia.net, Tel. 22836381, 22816713
- 7, Sovereign Park Apartments, 56-58, K. R. Road, Basavanagudi, Bangalore 560 004
  E-mail: vivabangalore@vivagroupindia.net, Tel. 26607409, 26607410
- 101-102 Mughal Marc Apartments, 3-4-637 to 641, Narayanguda, Hyderabad 500 029
  E-mail: vivahyderabad@vivagroupindia.net, Tel. 27564481, 27564482
- First Floor, Beevi Towers, SRM Road, Kaloor, Kochi 682 018, Kerala
  E-mail: vivakochi@vivagroupindia.net, Tel: 0484-2403055, 2403056

Published by arrangement with

Thorogood Publishers Limited
10-12 Rivington Street
London EC2A 3DU
UK

ISBN-10: 81-7649-371-6
ISBN-13: 978-81-7649-371-0

Published by Vinod Vasishtha for Viva Books Private Limited, 4737/23, Ansari Road, New Delhi 110 002. Printed and bound by Raj Press, R-3, Inderpuri, New Delhi - 110 012.

This book is based on Business Information Factsheets researched and written by enterprise and economic development agency Project North East. Chapter contributors include David Irwin, Linda Jameson, Andrew Maville and Bill Waugh all of whom work at Project North East. The introduction has been written and the text edited by Julie Lewthwaite.

The information is checked by independent experts to ensure, as far as possible, that it is accurate and up-to-date. However, neither the publishers nor the authors can accept any responsibility for any actions that you take based on its content. If you are in doubt about a proposed course of action, you should seek further professional advice.

Contents

Introduction

Successful negotiation

Introduction: Successful negotiation

'Negotiating' is a term used a great deal nowadays, in newspapers, on television and on radio. It often seems to imply that only large companies or whole countries are involved, not individuals. However, we all frequently have to negotiate, even though we may not actually realise it.

In fact, all human interactions are characterised by some sort of negotiation between or among people trying to give to and take from one another. This process of exchange is continual and often goes unnoticed. Take time for a moment to consider why you occupy the position that you now do. How much negotiation did it take – at home, at school, at work, elsewhere – to enable your occupation of this position? Negotiating may be thought of as a process of bargaining to reach a mutually acceptable agreement.

Good negotiating skills are essential to the smooth running of your business. You need to be able to negotiate with many different types of people in many different business situations – whether you are negotiating a loan from your bank manager or the next pay rise with a union or staff representative. The skills, once learned, will stand you in good stead.

It may help your negotiations if you understand the attributes of a good negotiator. Being good doesn't necessarily mean that you always come out on top in a negotiation – it means that you reach a conclusion that is satisfactory for your business. This might mean proceeding with a specific course of action or it may mean not proceeding because the terms are unacceptable.

My own organisation, for example, buys old buildings, refurbishes them and divides them into smaller units, which are let on an easy in, easy out basis to new and growing businesses. My colleague, who manages all this, has become an excellent negotiator. He assesses a building carefully, determining how much finance will be required to refurbish and convert it. He calculates the most we can afford to pay. He makes an offer some way below that amount. He is then willing to negotiate, but never exceeds his original calculation because he knows we would then lose money. If the vendor is happy to sell to us, everyone is happy. If the vendor can do better elsewhere, that's fine too.

Much has been said about so-called 'hard' negotiation – negotiating aggressively and getting your own way at all costs. The danger here is that you might win this time around, but at a potentially high cost. The other party may refuse ever to deal with you again; can you afford to destroy relationships in this manner?

It is arguably always better to look for a fair and mutually beneficial outcome; that way the door is left open for you to do business again in the future. You build, rather than break, relationships.

Negotiating fears

When we are negotiating – particularly if we are new to the situation or acting as lead negotiator for the first time – there will be much that makes us nervous. No matter how familiar you are with your subject, there are still pitfalls and perils when negotiating with an individual or a group of people. Things we might fear include:

- difficult questions that we struggle to answer;
- drying up – forgetting what to say;
- losing the attention of our counterparts, seeing them drift off and glaze over; and,
- not capturing their interest in the first place.

Being sufficiently well prepared will help overcome these fears and keep you in control.

Start by setting your objectives. Your objectives describe the intended outcome of the negotiation rather than the process itself. Their purpose is to let you know where you are going and to recognise when you have arrived. They allow the effectiveness of the negotiation to be evaluated after the event and allow you to select the most appropriate materials, approach and resources.

Your objectives might be quite complex, or might be expressed simply as, 'Get the contract'! It is a good idea to think about what you hope to achieve and to write that down before you start preparing.

There will be times when you are required to make a presentation, either formally or informally, perhaps as a prelude to, or as a part of, the overall negotiation process. Standing up in front of a group of people to speak is not something that comes easily to everyone; consequently thorough preparation is essential.

Think about how to illustrate your points – is it appropriate to use props or samples in order to get the message across? Avoid using anything so complicated that it makes you nervous, but where appropriate do give people samples to handle or to look at.

Before you stand up in front of an audience, you should practise thoroughly. If possible, make your presentation to your colleagues and get feedback from them. However you prepare, be sure that you have run through everything at least three times before the actual event.

It is generally a fact that no matter how nervous a situation may make us, we have to get on with it anyway. Consequently, we must try to control things in the best way we know how, and I would suggest that that way is the three Ps:

1. Prepare.
2. Practise.
3. Participate.

In other words, do as much as you can before the event, and don't be a bystander during it – get involved, say your piece, argue your point and make a difference. You may be surprised at how much more confident you will feel!

Making choices

Negotiation is largely about choice. What do you choose to offer or to concede, and what do you choose to accept or reject. Often the basis of a choice will be to solve a problem; you have reached an impasse in your negotiations and need to identify the best way forward. The word 'problem' is used deliberately here, because even if you are looking at an interesting opportunity for your company, your problem will be how to exploit that opportunity. On the other hand, you may really have a problem – your proposal was perceived to be insulting; your team have walked out so you cannot fulfil the order within the negotiated deadline; a key member of staff has just resigned; or, a competitor has started undercutting your prices. It should be remembered that in some instances, the best way forward will be quite simply to shake hands and walk away. There is nothing to be gained by striking a deal at all costs; it has to be mutually beneficial.

During the course of the negotiating process, you will face decisions to be taken or problems to be solved. Whilst you can anticipate problems during the preparation stage and formulate a strategy for dealing with them should they arise, you will inevitably have to think on your feet during the negotiation itself. If you are to come up with a solution, you must first be able to define the problem accurately. Once you are able to do this, you can begin to set objectives for the rest of the decision making process. Often these will be quite straightforward, but try not to be too constrained by what you've always done before.

Thinking creatively

In many cases the most logical course of action is not the best and by taking a more creative approach to a situation we can often come up with something much better.

Dr Edward de Bono, the originator of the concept of lateral thinking, is regarded by many as the leading authority on teaching creative thinking. He asserts that the simplest way to describe lateral thinking is to say; 'you can't dig a hole in a different place by digging the same hole deeper'.[1] In other words, you have to move sideways and look at

[1] Edward De Bono, *Serious Creativity*, HarperCollins

the problem from a different angle. Get a fresh perspective, get away from the same old train of thought. In negotiating terms, this could mean a change of strategy. That which worked with the last customer (or last two, or last ten) might not be appropriate or effective this time around.

A manufacturer of aeroplane tyres held a creative thinking session in order to generate ways of boosting business. The question they were considering was how to encourage more airlines to use their tyres. One of the people present suggested that they should give the tyres away – that way they'd all use them! Strange as it may seem, that was the approach adopted, resulting in the tyre company winning a considerable amount of business from its competitors. In time, the competitors followed suit.

Thinking laterally, the solution that was generated was that instead of selling airline tyres in the usual way, which represented quite a substantial cash outlay for the customer, they would give them the tyres and then charge them every time a plane took off and landed. This had benefits for both parties; the cost of tyres was spread over a longer period of time for the airline and the tyre manufacturer had a guaranteed and regular income. By thinking creatively, they found a different way to look at things. Rather than meeting with an airline that constantly tried to negotiate down the price of tyres, they took along a whole new approach to the negotiating process.

Creative thinking is also coloured by perception; true logic doesn't always see the long-term implications of a decision. An example quoted by Edward de Bono concerns little Johnny, an Australian five year old, whose friends offered him the choice of two coins, the $1 coin and the smaller $2. Little Johnny always took the larger coin. His friends thought him stupid for not realising that the smaller coin was worth twice as much as the one he chose and, whenever they wanted to make fun of him, they offered him the same choice and he took the same coin. An adult observed this little ritual one day and pointed out to Johnny that the smaller coin was actually worth more, to which little Johnny replied, 'Yes, I know that. But how often would they have offered me the choice if I had taken the $2 coin the first time?'

Human perception allowed little Johnny to make the choice he did – and, although it was a seemingly illogical choice, it paid off. The same could be applied to negotiating with prospective customers; do you want a one-off deal of $2 now, or would you rather have a dollar a week for the next six months? It pays us to use our ability to look at the big picture and perceive the possible results of our actions long-term.

Coping with criticism

When criticising someone else's suggestion or proposal or dealing with criticism of one of your own, always resist the temptation to make a personal attack – go for the ball, not the player. Beware of politics and personalities; you can rarely win if you enter those arenas. Keep all discussions firmly on a no-nonsense factual basis and deal with people fairly and rationally.

Criticism should be questioned – why is this not a viable proposal? Could it be that you or others are being constrained by the boundaries of rigid thinking? Perhaps there is a need for a more flexible approach. Also, whilst we should learn from our experiences, we should not make this an excuse to look back continually instead of looking forward.

Networking

Regard networking as an essential part of the process of marketing your business – and, by implication, a helpful pre-cursor to any negotiating requirement. Being in a position, for example, to bring in additional support or expertise may well help in ensuring a successful outcome. Networking is simply the active cultivation of useful contacts and the use of those contacts, when appropriate, to help in achieving required objectives. In most cases, those objectives are locating information and finding new customers.

Whilst networking is not a pre-requisite for successful negotiation, having a wide range of contacts often means that you can call on people for advice or assistance before undertaking a difficult negotiation.

Networking is something that a lot of people do without ever thinking about it, but if it is carried out as a deliberate activity it is much easier to control the results. Whilst chance encounters should never be ignored, it is not a good idea to rely solely upon chance as a way of building a comprehensive network of business contacts.

Seek out places where useful contacts might gather. Your local enterprise agency may know of, or organise, an enterprise club. The local Chambers of Commerce usually hold regular informal meetings for members, often based around informal talks followed by a buffet lunch. Don't be afraid to introduce yourself to people and discuss what both you and they do.

There may also be other fora that are specific to your industry or current business interests, such as regional branches of your trade association, professional institutions such as the Institute of Management, exporters' clubs, etc. These are usually designed specifically for the purpose of establishing contacts and exchanging information. Finally, don't forget any social or community activities in which you are involved. Organisations such as the Rotary Club have traditionally been seen as a fertile ground for networking purposes, but useful contacts may be found in many social scenarios.

Look for intermediaries who can make introductions, and don't forget friends – and friends of friends. Most people have a variety of friends, relatives and acquaintances, who in turn have their own circle of friends, etc. Within this comparatively close set of relationships it is astonishing how often you know somebody who knows somebody who can help – the difficulty lies in making the initial connection.

Finally, remember that networking is about communication and that communication is a two-way process. As well as using your network to gain information, use it to pass on any helpful little snippets that might come your way. People will appreciate your efforts and be more kindly disposed towards you if you have shown consideration to them.

Conclusion

Negotiating is a skill that impacts on all areas of life. You can negotiate good business for your company, you can negotiate satisfactory terms and conditions for you and your staff, and you can negotiate to get out of tricky situations, for example, if working relationships aren't going well.

Always look for the common ground and the area of mutual advantage. Don't try to get your own way at all costs; and take the long view – concentrate on developing relationships rather than destroying them.

So, what are the steps you can anticipate taking in a negotiation? What kinds of situations might call for your skills as a negotiator? And how can you make the most of each of them? This book considers and answers these questions, introducing the basic skills of negotiation and then describing a number of business situations in which those skills will be necessary.

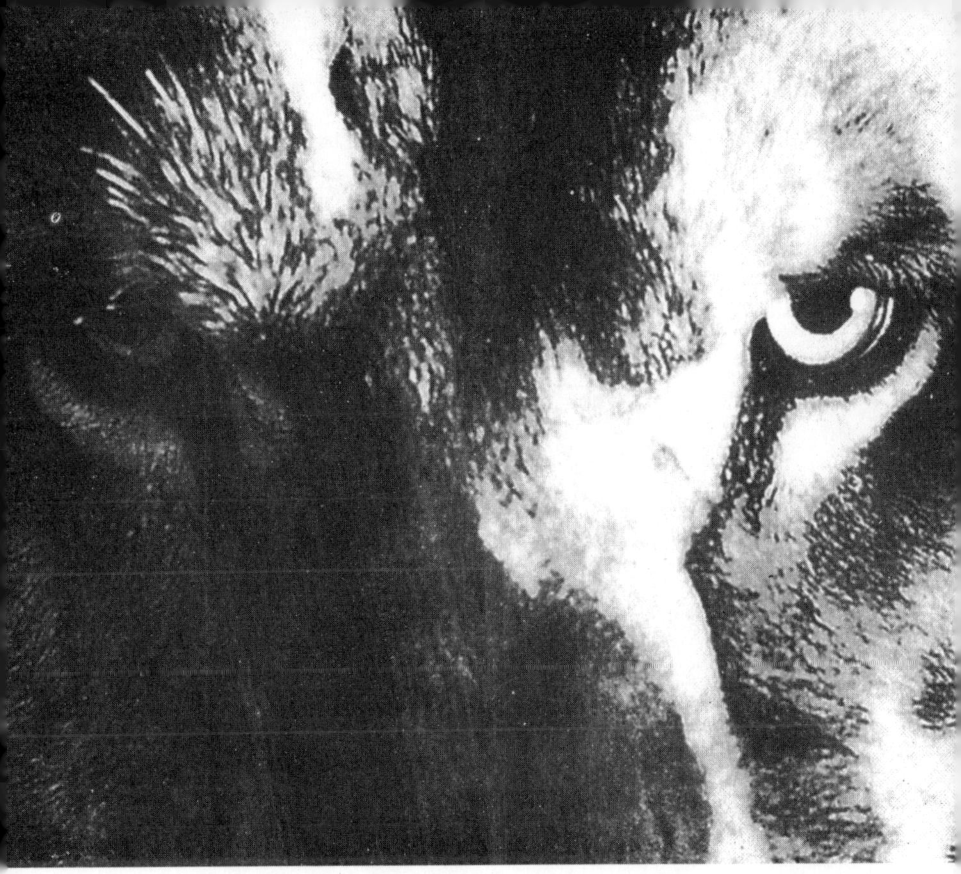

Part 1ONE

Useful skills for the negotiator

Chapter 1ONE

First steps in negotiation

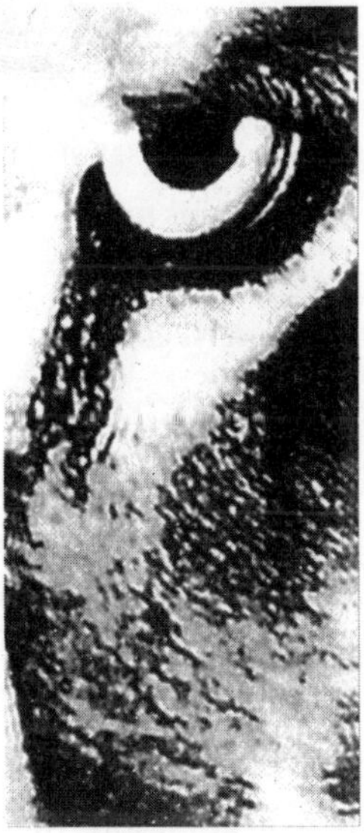

This chapter explains the key principles of the art of negotiating.

Introduction

An owner-manager of a small business, whether buying, selling or discussing employees' wages, must get the best possible deal without creating unnecessary conflict. Negotiations should be collaborative and constructive, satisfying both parties. If one party 'wins' at the other's expense, this may jeopardise future relations. However, there will, almost certainly, be occasions when you will find yourself in competitive negotiations. Negotiation skills can be learned and improved through use.

Important principles

Negotiating may be looked upon as the process of finding the point of balance between your own objectives and the objectives of the other party. Negotiations can be 'competitive' or 'collaborative'. In competitive negotiations the negotiator wants to 'win' even if this results in the other party 'losing'. It can end in confrontation. In collaborative negotiations the aim is to reach an agreement which satisfies both parties, ie to maximise mutual advantage.

There is no one right way to negotiate. Each person will develop a style which suits them. Your skills will develop with experience, but you can try to pick up the basics from books, training videos and short training seminars. To negotiate successfully it is necessary to learn how to:

- understand the importance of preparation;
- understand how to develop objectives for negotiations;

- understand the strategies, tactics and signals which may be used; and,
- assess realistically the chances of a successful outcome.

Steps in negotiation

In any successful negotiation you are concerned with three key elements as shown below.

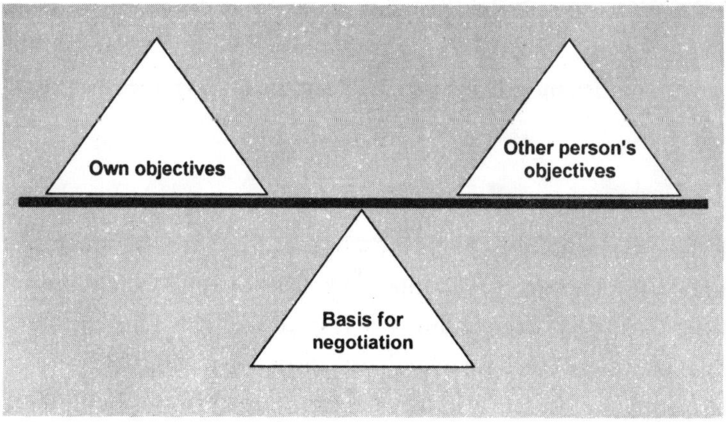

Figure 1: The three key elements to successful negotiation

Firstly, you need to know your own objectives. Then you need to plan and prepare for your negotiations. It is assumed that you have a thorough knowledge of the subject under negotiation. This will often be the case, for example, when dealing with customers or suppliers. However, you will also find yourself negotiating leases on property or loans from the bank and may not feel totally confident about your knowledge. You should try to find out as much information as possible, from various sources, prior to the meeting.

You may need to think about the procedure for the negotiation, particularly if there are a number of negotiable points.

If the negotiation is at your request, you will wish to retain control as far as possible to establish the scope for reaching agreement. It can be important, therefore, that you create a friendly atmosphere to achieve satisfactory negotiations.

Stages in negotiation

There are five essential stages in the negotiating process. Use the mnemonic 'Partners Don't Pick Bad Arguments' to remember them!

1. Prepare

Define your objectives. These must be specific, achievable and measurable. In other words, you must have a clear idea of what you want from the other party, you must be realistic and you must be able to assess how well you have done. Write them down. Objectives should also be put into order of priority. One way to do this is to classify them as 'must achieve', 'intend to achieve' and 'like to achieve'. For example, you have bought a photocopier for your office. It breaks down after a week and you have to contact the supplier. What are your objectives?

- Must achieve: the use of a photocopier that works.
- Intend to achieve: get the photocopier repaired.
- Like to achieve: get a replacement photocopier.

Research. Gather as much information as possible about the subject to be negotiated. The person with the most information usually does better in negotiations. For example, two people have each prepared a very important document. They both need to have them processed by the one desktop publishing operator in the firm and couriered to the destination for the following morning. But there is only time to have one job finished before the daily courier collection at 4pm, so the two argue over whose document is the most vital. If they argue too long neither job is finished on time and both would 'lose'. The senior could pull rank, resulting in the junior being the 'loser', and the possible loss of his future co-operation. If they obtained more information they would find out that the courier company runs an optional 6pm collection which also guarantees delivery before 11am the next day. A 'win/win' situation could be achieved.

2. Discuss

This is the process of exploring each party's needs, starting with tentative opening offers. These need to be realistic, otherwise there will be little scope for a satisfactory conclusion. If both parties are co-operative, progress can be made. If one side is competitive, problems may arise. Analyse the other party's reaction to what you say.

Use an opening statement covering the main issues at stake for each party. Allow the discussion to develop naturally. Make it clear that at this stage you just wish to talk, not negotiate as yet. Establish a relationship with the other person. Ask questions to find out more about their needs and to keep things moving. The more you find out about one another's needs, the greater the possibility that you will find a mutually acceptable solution.

3. Propose

This is the stage where you are giving and receiving proposals and suggestions. Remember to trade things, not just to concede to them. You'll find this phrase invaluable:

'If you (give us something), then we'll (give you something).'

Look for the opportunity to trade things which are cheap for you to give, but valuable to the other party, in return for things which are valuable to you. For example, Kevin is a painter and decorator who needs to rent a reasonably priced flat. Mr Smith is the landlord of a property which he is letting for £50 per week. The property is in relatively bad condition:

Mr Smith: 'The room is £50 per week.'

Kevin: 'That's a little more than I was expecting to pay.'

Mr Smith: 'There are lots of other people interested in the flat if you don't want it.'

Kevin: 'If you give me the flat for £40 per week, then I'll paint the walls in the living room for you .'

Mr Smith: 'If you paint the living room and the kitchen then I'll let you have the room for £40.'

Kevin: 'That's a deal.'

4. Bargain

After discussing each other's requirements and exchanging information, the bargaining can start (as in the example above). Generally speaking, you receive more if you start off asking for more, or will concede less if you start off offering less. If conflict arises at this point, indicate that your opening position is not necessarily what you will finally accept. Agreement is reached when both parties find an acceptable point somewhere between the starting positions.

In any negotiation, you quickly need to discover whether there is a likelihood that you might be able to reach a satisfactory agreement. This may be thought of graphically, as illustrated below, as an overlap of objectives. For example, a seller may be seeking to maximise the sale price, but has a price below which they must not go. Similarly, a buyer may want to minimise the purchase price, but will have a maximum above which they will not buy.

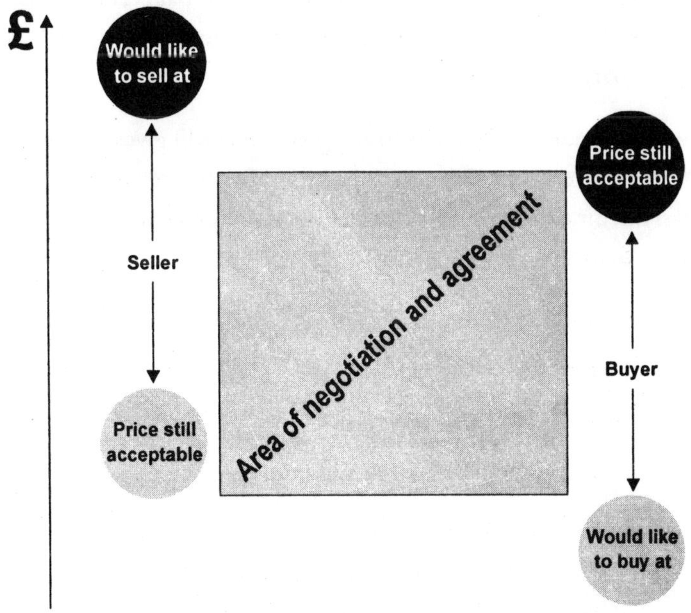

Figure 2: OVerlapping objectives leading to satisfactory agreement

When your offer is made, state it clearly. If you use words like 'approximately' or 'about', an experienced negotiator can challenge on a number of issues and change your offer dramatically.

When the other party's offer has been made, the next step is to find out exactly what it includes. Ask for clarification. You will have prepared a list of your requirements in the preparation stage, so ensure that these are met.

5. Agreement

When agreement is in sight, listen for verbal indications such as 'maybe' or 'perhaps'. Look for non-verbal signs, for example papers being tidied away. It is time to summarise what has been discussed and agreed. Do not start bargaining again.

Offer a summary of what has been agreed, this will give a chance to confirm any decisions. As soon as possible after the negotiation send a letter documenting the agreement. Having the agreement in writing is better than a handshake on the deal.

The letter should mention the following points:

- the terms of the agreement;
- the names of those involved;
- the prices mentioned plus discounts etc;
- individual responsibilities; and,
- time schedules and any deadlines agreed.

Post-mortem

We would suggest that as a matter of course you also conduct a post-mortem on the proceedings while they are fresh in your mind. Things to consider include:

- What went well? Why?
- What didn't go well? Why?
- Were you sufficiently well prepared?
- Did you question to gain information effectively?
- Did you use that information to guide your proposal?
- Were you happy with the outcome?
- What will you do differently next time?

Useful **tips**

1. Be assertive.
2. Be patient.
3. Be open minded.
4. Listen carefully.
5. Be self-disciplined.
6. Plan carefully and fully.
7. Be creative.
8. Be flexible.
9. Be persuasive.

10. Be decisive.
11. Show confidence.
12. Show consideration.

Chapter 2TWO

Approaches to negotiation

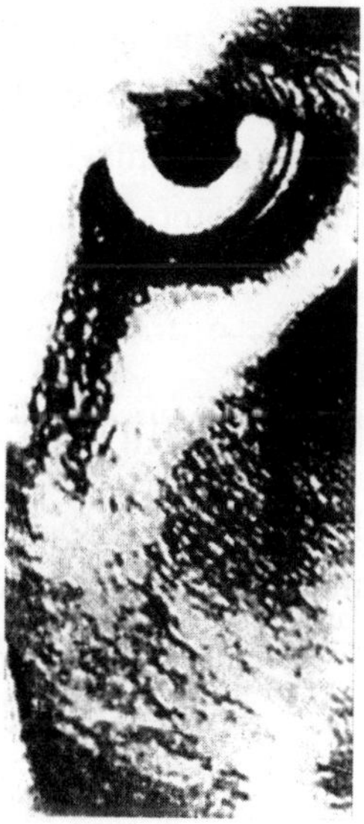

This chapter describes the alternative approaches to the process of negotiation.

Introduction

Styles of negotiating need to vary according to the circumstances and the people involved. Most negotiations will be a mixture of the collaborative and competitive approaches. It is generally more productive to steer the proceedings towards collaboration rather than competition.

Negotiating roles

Before we look at these approaches in more detail, let's look at the roles that you might take on in a negotiation. It is possible to identify five, each of which has particular strengths.

1. The factual negotiator

- Knows all the facts related to the negotiation.
- Asks factual questions.
- Covers all bases to ensure that no facts are left out.
- Provides information.

Factual negotiators tend to leave aside emotional issues such as 'face' – a person's desire for a positive identity. (People like to feel and look good and will react in a hostile manner to attacks that make them feel or look bad.) They can get most involved in details about the negotiation.

2. The relational negotiator

- Establishes relationships with the other party.
- Is sensitive to the other party's emotional issues.
- Builds trust.
- Perceives the position of the other party.

Relational negotiators can lose sight of the reasons for negotiation and the objectives, in their anxiety to build relationships. They can also give away information without realising it. Their sensitivity can make them become emotional and lose perspective.

3. The intuitive negotiator

- Comes up with unexpected solutions or ways of approach.
- Sorts the wheat from the chaff – the key issues from the irrelevant detail.
- Visualises the implications of a proposal.
- Accurately guesses the progress of negotiation.
- Sees the 'big picture'.

Intuitive negotiators can be dangerous because of their wildness and lack of discipline.

4. The logical negotiator

- Sets the rules of the negotiation.
- Develops an agenda.
- Argues in a logical rather than emotional way.
- Adapts their position to meet changing situations.

The logical negotiator can sometimes see the process of negotiation as being more important than the content or outcome.

5. The lead negotiator

Finally, all these approaches or roles need to be co-ordinated by the lead negotiator, who is responsible for all of the above roles and who makes the final decision about strategy, etc.

It is likely that you will exhibit some or all of these roles in your own negotiations. If your intuitive negotiator is strongest, you will need to develop discipline. If your logical negotiator is most prominent, you may need to develop relationship building skills.

Competitive negotiation

In the competitive approach, negotiations have an unfriendly atmosphere and each party is clearly out to maximise the benefit to themselves.

Opening: Avoid making the opening bid; it gives a great deal of information to the other party. If you encounter a competitive situation you should limit the information you give out and attempt to control the agenda.

Concessions: Conceding in a competitive situation is seen as a sign of weakness, so keep it to a minimum. The size of your first concession gives the opposing party an idea of your next best alternative, telling them exactly how far they can go.

Conflict: When conflict comes out into the open, use assertiveness skills to maintain your position and defuse the situation. Tactics can include the following:

- Make sure your position is strong and clear. Prepare well so that your arguments are well supported and to the point. The more relevant information you have the more effective your argument. Irrelevant arguments indicate weakness.
- Avoid attacking or threatening your opponent. Such behaviour may work in the short-term but to an experienced negotiator it indicates weakness. It can suggest desperation and the lack of an adequate alternative. Remember your objectives: 'must', 'intend' and 'like to' achieve.
- Work on the other party's real needs rather than their expressed desires. Information about this can be obtained from your research, listening skills and by observing body language. For example, an employee may be pushing hard for a pay rise to compensate for the fact that they feel overloaded with work. Focus on the source of the problem, and discuss solutions (eg, more forward planning, recruiting an assistant, etc).

Collaborative negotiation

Negotiation is often seen as a battle where the stronger party defeats the weaker party, ie 'win/lose'. In some cases negotiations can break down altogether (eg, in an industrial dispute which results in industrial action). Nobody wins, ie, 'lose/lose'. The collaborative approach is not based on conflict, but upon the belief by everyone involved that it is possible to reach a solution where everyone benefits, ie, 'win/win'. This approach tends to produce the best results, mainly because there is much better communication between the parties. In addition, it makes for better long-term relations if it is necessary to work together over a long period.

Opening: The opening will involve you gathering as much information as possible but also disclosing information so solutions can be developed that are acceptable to both parties. This can involve:

- considering many alternatives for each issue;
- using open questions (which don't have yes/no answers); and,
- helping the other party to expand his/her ideas about possible solutions.

Both parties will make concessions if necessary, normally aiming to trade things which are cheap for them to give but valuable to the opposing party.

If you listen, summarise, paraphrase and disclose (for example, 'I would like to ask you a question…' or 'I feel that I need to tell you that…') in collaborative negotiations, conflict will be kept to a minimum, enabling mutual advantage to be obtained.

Conclusion

Negotiation is a means of arriving at a solution to a problem in a manner which ideally results in an outcome which is of benefit to all parties; in other words, a win/win situation. Everybody is happy, and as a result of your different needs and objectives, it is possible for everyone to leave the table with substantial gains and inconsequential losses. The trick is to trade things which cost you little but which have a high value to the other party.

Negotiation calls for assertive behaviour. You should collaborate to achieve an agreement satisfactory to all concerned. If you deal with an aggressor, someone who always wants to win at all costs, then the result would be win/lose. The danger of taking this stance is that it may lead to a complete lack of co-operation – the other party dislikes and distrusts the aggressor's style, and so will not bargain – so that the final outcome is lose/lose. Needless to say this must be avoided, otherwise the process becomes pointless.

Useful **tips**

The following pointers will help you when planning your strategy and conducting your negotiation:

1. Be assertive.
2. Respect the other party – they have objectives, too.
3. Open with a realistic offer, be neither too greedy nor sell yourself too cheaply.

4 Work out your objectives in advance – this makes it easier for you to compromise if that becomes necessary.

5 Always trade – don't give anything for nothing.

6 If you need time to think, take it – ask for a short break and recap your notes. Don't be pushed into a decision you haven't thought through.

7 Make sure that the outcome is mutually beneficial and that all parties leave with a feeling of well-being; that way they'll be happy to do business with you again.

Chapter 3THREE

Creative bargaining

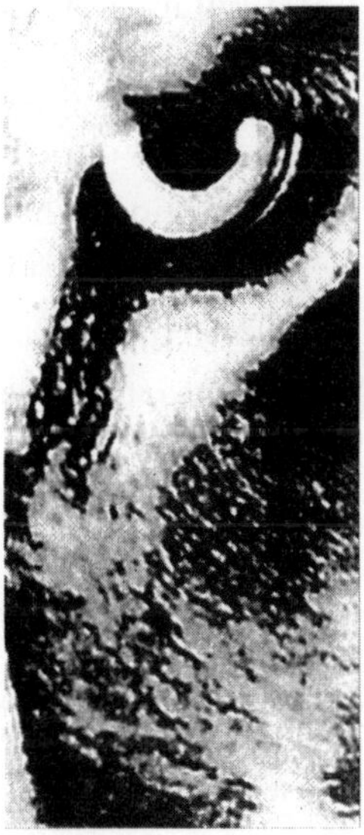

This chapter looks at methods of breathing new life into a negotiation and keeping it moving forward should you hit a stumbling block or run into a brick wall.

Introduction

We all have a sphere of experience or operation in which we feel at home – this is our comfort zone. Learning or doing something new takes us outside of that area and can feel unpleasant. However, it is only by leaving the constraints of the comfort zone that we can grow and develop. In time, areas once outside the comfort zone become incorporated into it and we can push out the boundaries once more.

It is a fact of life that the more you are involved in negotiation, the more likely you are to get stuck in a rut. This is unsurprising – you find a method of negotiation that works for you, and so you stick with it; you identify a deal that most people find attractive, so you offer it as a matter of course; you become familiar with a particular strategy, and so use it automatically.

Whilst this is undoubtedly a comfortable situation for you, there will be times when your standard strategy, for one reason or another, simply does not work. At those times in particular, like both little Johnny and the aeroplane tyre manufacturer in the introduction, you need to try a different tack.

What does your counterpart want?

If you hit a brick wall it could well be because you do not clearly understand what it is that your opposite number is trying to achieve. Whilst all parties should, and most likely will, set objectives prior to negotiation as part of their preparation, they are unlikely to share their objectives with one another. Consequently, if you second guess someone's motives or desired outcomes and get it wrong, your best effort at a mutually acceptable solution may be doomed to failure from the start.

The best thing to do in such circumstances is simply to ask the other party what their objectives are. Having said that, there are more subtle ways than just saying, 'So, tell me – what is it you want, then?' It is arguably better to gather information through discussion and then take a step-by-step approach, clarifying points one by one. For example:

- 'So, as I see it, your main concern is IT support to install the software…'

  'Yes.'

- 'And you are also keen to have sound technical support for the term of the contract…'

  'That's right.'

- 'In addition, you are looking for a discount against the purchase of a multi-user licence…'

  'Right again.'

And so on. There are four main benefits to this course of action:

- you focus the other party's attention on the facts;
- you confirm your true understanding;
- you identify any areas of misunderstanding; and,
- you enhance the confidence of the other party in your ability to strike a satisfactory agreement.

Offer options

Another useful tactic is to increase the number of variable options available. It is a good idea to have a list of things (even if only mentally) that are cheap for you to offer but which are sufficiently desirable to the other party that they add value to the proposal. For example, if you obtain a two or three year commitment to a product or service, you could offer a discount as your income is then guaranteed for that length of time. If a contract has to be negotiated annually, you will possibly have to offer a discount to get business in subsequent years anyway.

Alternatively, you could offer an enhanced after sales service (peace of mind for the other party, whereas if you are confident of the quality of your product or service, at little or no cost to you); or a discounted price on a second product (it's all additional profit by this stage).

The bargaining stage of negotiation would be where you work through your possible variables and design a winning package for the deal. Be alert to responses from the other party that signal interest; if you are confident that you are really on the right track, then you can proceed with more confidence.

Be creative

Apply creative thinking to the situation. Try to see it from the other person's point of view. Walk around the problem and look at it from a different angle. Perhaps you can spot something new that will offer a way forward.

If you are part of a negotiating team, then you could brainstorm opportunities. In the first stage of brainstorming – the ideas generation stage – anything goes. No criticism is allowed, no matter how crazy the ideas seem. You do not want to stem the creative flow or to make people afraid to offer up their suggestions in case their ideas are ridiculed.

Stage two is the evaluation stage – weed out the no-hopers (generally those that come into the categories of immoral, illegal or impossible) and discuss and explore the other suggestions fully. Be sure that you do discuss potential ways forward thoroughly; whilst this is an evaluation of the ideas on the table and is therefore based on logic and common sense, it is still important that you be open minded and creative in your approach.

One way or another a negotiation requires closure; if no way forward can be found, then closure will mean walking away from the situation. Whilst there are times when this is undoubtedly the only option because your negotiations cannot come up with a deal that matches the Best Alternative To a Negotiated Agreement (BATNA) of one or other of the parties, this is only acceptable when all avenues have been explored. Leave no stone unturned in your search for a method of kick-starting a stalled negotiation.

Take the long-term view

If you are the buyer rather than the seller and someone is insisting that they cannot be flexible (on price, for example) help them to see the long-term view. This may be the first deal you have negotiated, but how much might your business be worth over two, five or even ten years? You are both exploring the possibility of establishing a business relationship; if the foundations are solid, then you could build on it for a long time to come.

Conclusion

In negotiation, as in so many other situations, it can pay you to move outside of your comfort zone. If you allow yourself to be constrained by what has gone before you could miss out on opportunities that have potentially valuable outcomes for your company.

Before you even get into the arena of proposal and counter proposal, however, make sure you fully understand the needs of the other party.

Be open-minded and look for reasons why something can be achieved rather than reasons why it can't. 'How can we..' or 'Why can't we…' will prove to be useful openers to questions used when looking to close the gap between the proposal and the desired outcome of the other party.

Useful **tips**

1. Don't get stuck in a rut – just because something has worked before doesn't mean it's right this time around.
2. Offer options – preferably that are cheap for you to supply yet add value for the other party.
3. Be creative – see the situation from a different angle.
4. Accept that there are times when you must walk away – but be confident if you do that there genuinely was not an alternative course of action.
5. Take the long-term view – look at the lifetime value of the business relationship.

Chapter 4FOUR

Dealing with pressure

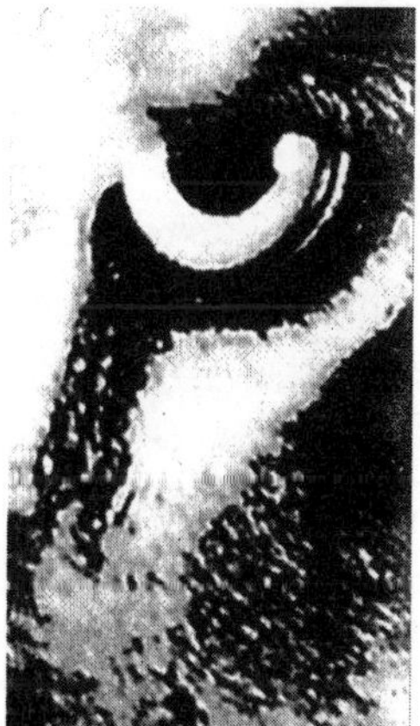

Difficult negotiations will always be stressful, so it will help to understand techniques for reducing stress. This chapter discusses stress and introduces some of the better known methods for dealing with it.

Introduction

Working under pressure is very stressful, so leading a 'normal' family life is difficult. You often need to work late and at weekends. You may feel unable to take holidays. Dealing with staff problems can be particularly stressful. If business is not good, the uncertainty also adds to the stress. It is very important not to get into a vicious cycle where anxiety begins to affect your performance, in turn creating more anxiety and so on. Stress can be positive, even stimulating, but too much, over a long period, can become a real problem. It is important to recognise this and take positive action. Find out how to relieve your stress and organise your life to minimise the problem. If necessary, get professional advice. Watch for signs of stress in your staff and help them to deal with it.

Symptoms of stress

Stress is a physical reaction to a threatening situation: heart rate, blood pressure and breathing rate increase. You perspire more and your muscles tense up. In the short-term, energy levels increase, but in the long-term you can become exhausted and lose weight. Links between stress and illness are well established. The list includes heart disease, strokes, kidney damage and disturbance of blood sugar levels.

Many people thrive under stress. They are able to use stress reactions to their advantage. Even so, they may still have medical problems in the long-term. For most people, stress is extremely debilitating and prevents them from functioning to their full potential. In critical situations you become nervous and embarrassed. Instead of thinking clearly, you become preoccupied with negative thoughts. It is hard to make decisions. Concentration declines and you can become forgetful.

Working with someone showing signs of stress can be difficult. They can become very negative, pessimistic, overly sensitive to criticism and aggressive. Creativity is stifled. Self-esteem can disappear. Over a prolonged period there is the danger of serious depression.

Stress build up

Some stress is focused around a particular event or crisis. Stress can also build up gradually, over a long period of time. Various factors can contribute to the build up. Some stressful events in life are obvious, such as bereavement, divorce, moving house, starting a new job, dismissal, etc. It is important to understand all your sources of anxiety. Watch for times when a number of stressful events coincide and plan accordingly.

Make a list of the things that cause you most anxiety. Look at each in turn. On its own, each worry looks less formidable. Make a realistic assessment of the worry. Why does it concern you? Are you being reasonable? Are the consequences you imagine likely to happen? If it is a genuine worry, are you going to do anything about it? If not, why let it bother you? Most importantly, can you rationalise things? Are you trying to do too much?

Stress can build up in the course of the day. It is important to understand how you function during the day. For example, if you are a morning person, do the stressful things early. Build in breaks throughout the day. It is all too easy to keep going when you feel strong. Discipline yourself to stop and relax regularly, before you feel the need. If you do this, you will actually achieve more and be less inclined to run out of steam towards the end of the day.

Unrealistic expectations and standards

A common cause of stress comes from having unrealistic expectations about what you can achieve. It is easy to overestimate what can be done in the course of one day. If you set impractical targets for business success you could be condemning yourself to overwork for the indefinite future. For a perfectionist, the ordinary untidiness of everyday life can be a constant source of irritation. If you expect to do everything perfectly, you put yourself under unnecessary pressure – it is simply not possible. Similarly, if you can't tolerate fallibility in others, you will create unnecessary tension amongst staff. For many, being under stress is an important part of their identity, a way to show that they are important and dynamic. However, people must recognise their limitations. By overdoing things you become less effective; if you work within your limitations you will be more effective in the long run.

Accepting your stress

Attitudes to work and life can't be changed overnight. It is important to be realistic and to accept that there is a limit to what can be achieved. This applies to the way you tackle stress too. If you are the sort of person who suffers from stress, you will always suffer from it to some extent. However, you can take positive action to minimise stress and its effect upon you. Stress is an important part of life. It can often be channelled to your advantage. Some people believe that you can overcome ('unlearn') many of your fear reactions, but this does take time. It is worth tackling your negative feelings. With experience, you will be able to overcome them in many situations.

Planning ahead

Good forward planning is very effective in countering stress. Long-term plans should be realistic in terms of what you, and your team are capable of. This also applies to your daily action plans. Tackle unpleasant tasks as soon as possible, before they become a source of worry. Be imaginative about planning rest and relaxation into your life. If faced with a particularly challenging event, plan and prepare well in advance. Anticipate problems and how to counteract them, but above all, have faith in the decisions that you take.

Dealing with people

A common source of stress is anxiety about dealing with people, especially anticipating conflict. Assertiveness training can make you more confident in dealing with people and in facing conflict. You can't keep everyone happy all the time. Assess the demands being made upon you. Can they be reduced or adapted to suit better your capacity? Accept that you will fail to deliver on some occasions. Learn to delegate. If you can't ask others to do things for you, you will be overloaded with work.

Relieving the symptoms

Everyone is different. There is no single best way to fight stress. Different pressures affect people in different ways. It is important to understand how stress affects you as an individual.

Talking

It is easy to get things out of proportion. Talking things over with friends or colleagues can help you get things into perspective. The process helps to release some of the stress that might be bottled up. It also helps you to think things through and to find a solution. It may be hard to talk on this level. Work to develop relationships which allow you to make your worries known and to get (and to give) positive support. Small business clubs are a good place to meet others who understand the pressures that you face. It can also help to discuss possible approaches in advance. For example, if you will be conducting a difficult negotiation, brainstorm with friends or partners the possible responses of the other party and rehearse your own reactions.

Relaxation

It's easy for someone to say 'relax', but actually doing it when you feel stressed is another matter. There are many relaxation techniques; most include some of the following:

- Stand up, stretch and loosen your muscles.
- Sit, or lie in a comfortable position in a quiet place where you won't be disturbed.
- Gently try to turn your mind to a peaceful thought, eg, a calm sea, or a sunset. Think of a place and time when you felt particularly relaxed and imagine yourself there.
- It may help to repeat a peaceful word such as 'relax' inwardly.
- Let your breathing become slow, deep and rhythmical.
- Go through each part of your body in turn (eg, left foot, left leg, right foot, etc), tense and relax each muscle group until the whole body is relaxed.
- Continue to relax, breathing deeply and thinking peaceful thoughts for a few minutes.

Such methods work more or less effectively, depending on how stressed you are. It is better do this type of exercise two or three times a day, and not just when your stress has built up to a high level. To do this properly you may need some coaching from an expert.

Exercise

Stress is essentially a physical reaction to some kind of threat, gearing you up for 'fight or flight' – something that the business environment gives you little scope to release. It is easy to lose sight of how much time we spend sitting at a desk. Much of our activity is 'small muscle' such as, talking, writing, typing, etc. This gives an insufficient outlet for your body's physical response. 'Large muscle activity' such as a short walk (if only to the other end of the office) or stretching and basic exercise movement helps to release this extra energy removing some of the adrenaline build up. Vigorous exercise, especially if it is non-competitive, (eg, running, cycling, swimming) is particularly helpful. Exercise and a healthy diet will help the body cope with stress.

Stimulation and balance

It is all too easy to think that your business is 'all important'. If you focus your life entirely around work, the fears and anxieties surrounding it become exaggerated. If other things occupy your mind, problems at work can be somewhat diluted. If you are too work focused, you risk losing touch with others on a social level. Having fun and enjoying things outside of work are very important for relieving stress. Socialising and active recreation are vital to recharge your batteries and to discharge stress. Above all, make sure you take a holiday every year.

Useful **tips**

1. Don't panic! Stress is a natural reaction to pressure. Be positive. Stress reactions can be reduced with practice and planning.

2. Get an outlet for your stress that suits you. Excessive smoking and drinking is not advisable.

3 If you let stress get to you it will affect your business. Talk to your business counsellor and, if necessary, see your doctor before things get too much.

4 Pay attention to the working environment, especially if you work with computers. If it is uncomfortable this will add to stress.

5 Read more about stress management. If possible get some training. There are a great many different methods and strategies for dealing with stress, far more than can be covered here. Find an approach that suits you.

Part 2TWO

People issues

Chapter 5FIVE

Relational influence and power

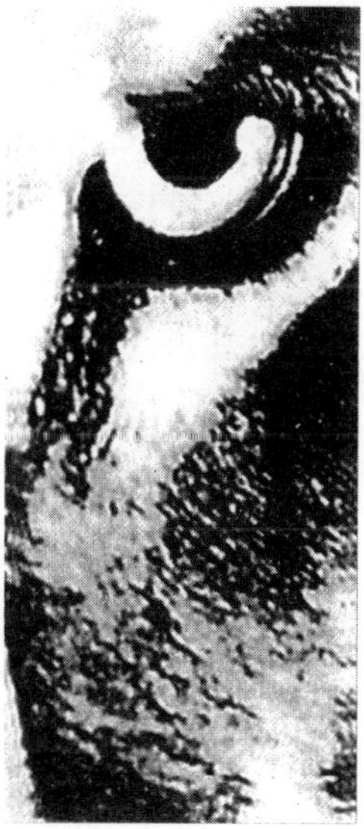

This chapter is about power within relationships and how to understand and use the knowledge to your advantage.

Introduction

The quality of a negotiation depends upon two things; the quality of the basic relationship between the parties involved and the quality of the communication that takes place. A good relationship with good communication between parties should enable successful negotiation. A poor relationship with poor communication is unlikely to amount to much.

The nature of a relationship in turn has an impact upon the quality of communication within it. If we do not trust someone, we are in danger of either disregarding what they say or looking for hidden meanings that may or may not actually exist. The nature of a relationship impacts heavily upon negotiation and is a major influencing factor on the likelihood of satisfactory outcomes. Consequently we are going to look at relationships from another angle – that of power – and see how this new viewpoint is likely to have an effect on negotiating tactics.

When we become aware of something or someone for the first time, we enter into a relationship with that thing or person. Relationships can be simple – your relationship with someone who serves you in a shop, or complex – your relationship with your mother. As relationships become more complex, they can be identified by a growing degree of dependence – in other words, how much we need whoever or whatever it is.

'Dependence' is different from 'liking': you might like the person you chat with occasionally on the bus or in the supermarket, but you do not need them; however, you might thoroughly dislike your boss and yet depend upon that person for guidance and support and, ultimately, for your livelihood. Similarly, you might not like the person with whom you are conducting negotiations one little bit, and yet be dependent on them for information, co-operation and agreement.

Dependence can be hard to admit because it defines vulnerability. It sketches out the invisible arena within which we must operate because crossing the line can be risky – your boss might discipline or sack you, your fellow negotiator might withdraw from the discussion. Of course we all have others who are dependent upon us, but is usually our own dependence – our own vulnerability – that we find difficult to confront and to accept.

Like it or not, however, dependence, vulnerability, and consequently power are influencing factors in all relationships. You might feel that you control the power balance, that you are subject to it or that it is equal. Nevertheless, it exists and it is a major influencing factor.

Types of power

French and Raven,[2] two sociologists, identified eight types of power in research that they carried out in the 1950s.

1. Positional power

This type of power comes from one person's position in relation to another. For instance, a manager may have power because of the position that he or she occupies, whereas a supervisor may have less power

---

[2] J. R. P. French and B. H. Raven, *The Bases of Social Power in Studies for Social Power*, D. Cartwright (Ed.), Institute for Social Power, 1959

because of the way in which people perceive their relative positions. Bear in mind that the people who are subject to it award this type of power to the person in question. Positional power is characterised by a need for the relationship to continue.

2. Information power

As individuals, the more information that we have, the more we feel able to control what is going on about us. This form of control involves one person having more information than another and using it to control the other person's uncertainty. People can become dependent upon others because of their need to control their own uncertainty.

3. Control of rewards

This is about having the power to reward for desired performance or behaviour. This type of power creates dependency upon the person giving the reward.

4. Coercive power

This is about having the power to punish for failure to behave in a desired fashion. This type of power is also likely to create dependency. People can depend on not being punished as well as depend on being rewarded.

5. Alliances and networks

This is an extended form of information power together with positional power.

6. Access to and control of agendas

If a person or an organisation can control the agenda in a negotiating situation, they can effectively set the ground rules. This means that they can legislate for the introduction of items that are favourable to themselves and for items that are unfavourable to be blocked. If the agenda is controlled, one of the parties to a relationship can be dependent upon the other to explain the rules for communication and subsequently negotiation.

7. Control of meaning and symbols

This type of power is one whereby one party will dominate the other by means of their use of language or the setting in which the relationship takes place. The legal system is a system that uses control of meaning to a great extent with its own language and many arcane symbols to support its power. Bank managers and solicitors use this type of power to some extent also. Consider the setting of your bank manager's office and the content of your discussions.

8. Personal power

This type of power may also be called 'referent' power. It is the type of power that springs from wanting to be like someone, because you feel that they have some desirable quality or qualities.

Using power

All negotiation is about power. Because there are always power imbalances in a relationship, negotiation goes on all the time. No matter what your overall approach to negotiation, you may need to consider the nature of power. Remember that the power in the relationship will influence the negotiation process and that negotiation is not limited to a formal 'across the table' session.

It is, of course, very rare that you will find that there is only one type of power in a relationship. In the case of a bank manager for example, he or she is likely to have six or seven of the types of power listed above. Once you've identified the types of power that are involved in the relationship, you can cast your strategy in a way that will help you work successfully in that relationship.

Let's carry the bank manager analogy a bit further. They have positional power and information power, at least about the bank's lending policies and possibly about similar organisations to yours. They will have reward power and conceivably coercive power, although this is likely to be illusory. They will have access to alliances and networks, and control of agendas through demands for a business plan. They will certainly have control of meaning and symbols in the form of their office setting and the way in which they dress.

Much of this power is dependency inducing. You will be dependent upon a bank manager for his knowledge of the bank's lending policies, his ability to reward or to coerce if you have already been rewarded. Where he controls the agenda, you will be dependent upon him to explain the rules.

Some people assert that negotiation is about developing strategies that will decrease or increase the dependency of one of the parties in a negotiation. The bank manager will use strategies that will attempt to increase the customer's dependency, whether or not he or she is a borrower. The customer should use strategies that reduce his or her dependence on the bank. These can correspond to the power strategies that the bank manager may wittingly or unwittingly use.

- **The first** type of strategy is knowing the area in which you are going to negotiate. If you are asking for money, the more you know both about the current state of the lending market and the particular scheme for which you are seeking money, the less dependent you will be upon the bank manager.
- **The second** is to maintain flexibility in your commitment to one bank. Banks will, within certain limits, protect themselves by exchanging information about classes of customer. This does not mean that you should not approach as many sources of finance as possible. If a bank manager is aware that you are not dependent on him, your negotiating position will be much stronger.
- **The third** is to develop your own networks and alliances. When a bank manager knows that you know other people in the area in which you propose to work, your potential dependency upon him as the only source of finance or information is reduced.
- **The fourth** is to manipulate rewards so that the manager will feel good about helping you. You may have rewards in your power that you do not use or realise that you have. People can feel rewarded when they are involved in an obviously successful project for which they can expect to receive praise. The bank manager is not immune to rewards.

- **The fifth** is to manipulate meaning and symbol yourself. Your first meeting with a bank manager is likely to be on his territory. Respond by inviting him to a second meeting on yours. Set a stage for his visit.
- **The sixth** is to use your own personal power. If you appear confident and relaxed, whilst committed to your project, you may be able to induce a manager to help you because of this.

Conclusion

Power may be real or illusory. Try to ascertain the extent of actual power held by the other party. The fact is that if you accept illusory power as real, then it is real for you.

Try not to be intimidated by the setting in which you find yourself. Much power may be created simply by setting the stage and whilst you should be prepared to use this tactic to your own advantage, you should beware of having it used against you by others.

Even if you think you hold the whip hand, aim for collaborative rather than competitive negotiation. 'Win/win' is the best outcome for all concerned.

Useful **tips**

1. Aim for collaborative rather than competitive negotiations.
2. Be aware of the power balance in the relationship and use it to your advantage.
3. Having understood the relationship, work to develop it.
4. Work to improve your own skills as a communicator.
5. Set clear objectives and goals at the outset.

Chapter 6SIX

Negotiating with integrity

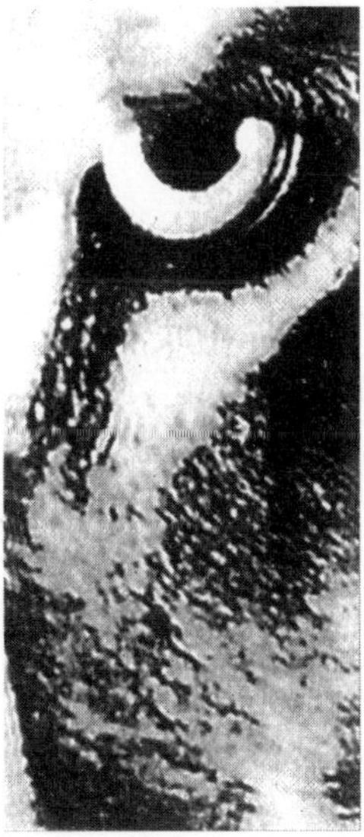

This chapter is about the way you behave during the negotiation process and the impact which that behaviour can have.

Introduction

When you become involved in a negotiation, it is desirable that you treat your opposite number with respect and that you do not compromise your personal integrity. In essence, this means that you should not:

- lie;
- be aggressive;
- be dismissive of the other party;
- use sarcasm; or,
- use threatening or intimidating behaviour.

Of course, the fact that you choose to eschew such behaviour is no guarantee that your opposite number will do the same. Consequently as well as considering the pitfalls of such behaviour, we will also look at methods of dealing with it should you be on the receiving end.

Tell the truth

Even if not the whole truth. Whilst it might be prudent to offer information only as and when it is relevant or necessary, you should not tell outright lies to your counterpart.

Remember that as well as not lying, you should be seen to be not lying. Bear in mind the image you are presenting to the other person. Try to see yourself as they see you – would you believe what you were being told? Body language tells us a great deal about other people. Often we take in the information subconsciously and we can make snap judgements based upon what other people's body language tells us. Remember that for each of us, perception is reality. If I believe that you are lying to me, all the truth in the world won't prevent me from feeling uneasy when doing business with you or from instinctively doubting your word.

The other side of the coin, of course, is whether your counterpart is (or whether you believe he is) lying to you. Should you find yourself in this situation, do bear in mind that you could be mistaken. It is a good idea to look for a number of indicators all pointing in the same direction and not just to base your opinion on one isolated example. Someone who appears fidgety and anxious might indeed be pulling the wool over your eyes; there again, they might be dying for a cup of tea or a cigarette!

If you wish to confirm or disprove your suspicions, question on points you either know or can quickly and easily verify as a 'test' first of all. If you still don't trust him, move on to more detailed matters.

If you find you were mistaken, you can simply move the negotiation forward. If you find you were right, you must begin to clarify everything point by point – and be sure to confirm it all in writing. Whilst it may be sufficient on the face of it to simply shake hands on a deal – a gentleman's agreement – it is good practice to get everything in writing; after all, someone who thinks it is acceptable to lie to your face is certainly not a gentleman.

Dealing with aggressors

When faced with aggression, the natural reaction is either to give as good as you get – fight – or to get out of there as quickly as possible – flight. Unfortunately, neither reaction is acceptable or even possible, on some occasions, in a business situation. Consequently we must have a strategy for understanding and dealing with aggressors.

Aggressive people are dealing from an emotional standpoint; the trick is not to meet emotion with emotion as this simply adds fuel to the flames, but to use logic and reason instead. Avoid 'absolute' statements as the result will be deadlock and possible lose/lose. Be prepared to justify your proposals and clarify objectives; at the same time be prepared to make concessions that cost you little but add value for the other party. If aggressors feel they are making headway and getting at least some of what they want, then their aggression is likely to be tempered. Remember that perception is reality, so even if you are calling the shots and making allowances, they will still feel good about what they believe they have gained.

At all times be alert for opportunities to move the negotiation forward and invite the aggressor to help you, perhaps by asking someone to join the discussion or by moving on to another item on the agenda on which agreement might more easily be reached. If he concedes to this, then you have struck a bargain and psychologically this should help towards striking more bargains.

Don't be beaten into a submissive stance; if all else fails, you can walk away. By this, we don't necessarily mean back off and call it a day, that really is a last resort. You could suggest that you negotiate with someone else in the organisation, or that you leave things for a couple of days and then fix up another meeting. An aggressor who realises that you can't be bullied may well be encouraged to behave more reasonably; after all, if his company is serious about doing business with you, can he afford to fail?

Being disrespectful

You must be very careful not to hurt people's feelings during negotiation. Such behaviours as not listening, talking over people, denying them even the smallest courtesies and so on can do enormous damage to a business relationship. By behaving in this manner you are attacking the other person's self-esteem. They will not wish to repeat the experience.

Remember that people are often quite sensitive, especially where their perception of their own skills and abilities as a businessperson is concerned. Consequently, if you disclose, following a negotiation, that if your counterpart had only tried a little harder you would have offered a bigger discount, don't be surprised if he avoids doing business with you again.

If you are on the receiving end of someone else's disrespect, try first and foremost not to take it personally. This is much easier said than done, but remember that your counterpart is being competitive and quite likely only playing the game as s/he sees it and feels it should be played.

The trick is not to rise to the bait. As far as possible, simply ignore the goading. If you are constantly being talked over, say, 'If I might finish my point…' and carry on. Be patient and be polite; very often by behaving properly yourself, you prompt similar behaviour in others.

If things reach an extreme point, you could challenge your counterpart by pointing out that s/he is not behaving fairly and asking if there is a reason for such behaviour. Keep your voice tone even and do not display aggression. Very often this is all that is needed to remedy the situation. Bullies do not like to be challenged and such behaviour is a form of bullying.

Using sarcasm

Sarcasm can be funny in the right circumstances and very tempting to use in many more. It should be strenuously resisted in negotiating situations, however, as it is a form of disrespect.

People who use sarcasm are perceived as being aggressive. Consequently those on the receiving end will be prompted to fight or flight. Either way, the negotiation is unlikely to be successful and you may find yourself in the middle of an increasingly unpleasant encounter as each successive sarcastic comment becomes more barbed and personal.

Beware also the more subtle forms of sarcasm; constantly asking 'Why?' questions can appear to be sarcastic – 'Why did you think that would be a good idea?' or 'Why would we want to pay that price?' – and it also undermines and belittles people. If someone is questioned on every point and made to feel stupid to boot, then the chances of developing a positive, long-lived and mutually beneficial business relationship are, to say the least, slim.

The same rules apply when dealing with sarcasm as with disrespect. Simply refuse to rise to the bait. If you believe a question, even if asked sarcastically, is worth answering, then go ahead and do so. Watch your voice tone and choice of language, however; do not join in the game of one-upmanship. If you believe a question is simply an excuse to have a go or is a red herring, you can choose to ignore it. Either respond with a question of your own or make a relevant point you wished to make anyway. Politicians do this all the time and with a little practice you could find this to be a useful tool.

Threatening behaviour

Even in competitive negotiation the rule is that you should avoid attacking or threatening your counterpart except as an absolute last resort.

Threats to use power may work in the short-term, but you send potentially dangerous messages when you threaten. The first is that your negotiating position is one which does not have an adequate alternative. Unless you have an alternative to a negotiated settlement, your position will be perceived as weak by an experienced negotiator. Threats communicate your desperation and can bring the negotiation to an end.

This is true in all circumstances – even if you are dealing with a client whose account is overdue and negotiating a method of payment, threats are pointless. Honest people would pay if they could and will be very worried by your behaviour; habitual debtors won't give two hoots either way.

If people threaten you, you have two main choices. The first is simply to ignore it and to stick to the facts. The second is to ask for clarification of exactly what they mean. By all means take notes as you get more information; the threat is most likely a bluff and by doing this you let your counterpart know that you know it is a bluff. Do not respond with sarcasm or anger, simply take things at face value and use factual language.

Conclusion

When you are faced with bad behaviour of whatever kind, you should simply refuse to accept it. You can do this either by ignoring it or, as with threats, by questioning for clarification of meaning. The fact that you behave fairly and correctly will often encourage other people to do the same. Should someone be downright abusive, then use your judgement and knowledge of your employer to help you to decide how to handle it. In fairness, few employers would wish their staff to be subjected to such treatment.

Useful **tips**

1. Be as honest and open as is wise.
2. Do not react to provocative behaviour.
3. Do not treat your opposite number with disrespect.
4. Threats rarely work – and if you make them, you must follow them through or lose credibility.
5. At all times, act according to your own personal code.

Chapter 7SEVEN

Negotiating globally

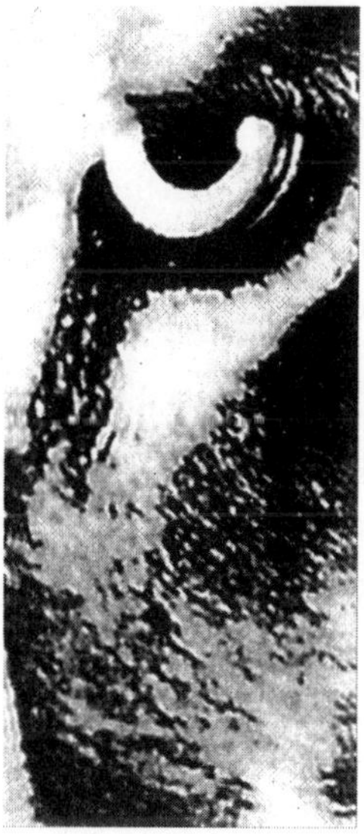

This chapter is about the need to understand ritual and culture in order to make people of other nationalities more comfortable when negotiating with you.

Introduction

In today's multi-cultural society, you may not even have to deal abroad to need to understand the ritual and culture of another society. Many companies in the UK have settled here from overseas and strive to maintain their native beliefs and traditions. Happily, the concepts involved in negotiating globally remain the same no matter where they are used.

If you are established in an industry and are dealing with people who are essentially your peers, then you will find negotiations very comfortable. You know pretty much what to expect and you can be confident that your own behaviour (based on honesty, openness and integrity) will raise no eyebrows.

You may have a few issues over rituals – this would be based on the 'culture' of the company with which you are dealing, culture in this instance being 'the way we do things around here'. Some companies expect staff always to wear a jacket to a meeting or when walking around the building; for others, shirtsleeves are the norm. In some organisations, staff are habitually five minutes late for meetings; in others, punctuality is essential. Global culture, however, would not be an issue.

Should you find yourself negotiating with either a company abroad or a company who have moved to the UK to do business, but who still maintain their native culture, you may not find things quite so straightforward.

Different nationalities have different values and ways of behaving. The Germans value logic and order. The Chinese discuss only those issues on a pre-agreed agenda. The Italians are very forthright if they feel they have cause to complain. Of course, these are stereotypical statements and viewpoints and the world isn't so clear cut, but as general rules of thumb then such statements are generally accurate. The same may be applied to home; saying that the British stoically bear bad service, for example, is generally true.

Build a model

In order to understand a different culture, you need information. Simply mimicking a few rituals that you have observed is unlikely to be enough of a basis on which to found a lasting business relationship – although as a starting point it is certainly better than encouraging people simply to be more English or totally ignoring the differences between cultures. A good way to approach a new culture is to follow a three stage, cyclical process: observe, analyse, and act accordingly.

Observe

Step one in observation might be to conduct some research into the country of origin of the people with whom you will be dealing. Check out the basics, such as size, population, religion, economic situation and so on. The fact that you can converse intelligently regarding the homeland of your counterparts shows that you have done your homework and wish to make the business relationship a success. You can also pick up 'cross-culture' books that will warn you off making some of the more obvious errors, such as not putting money directly into the hand of a Korean, for example (it's considered to be rude).

It is also a good idea to learn a few words of the language. You may not be expected to be fluent, but if you can greet people and say 'please' and 'thank you' in their language, then your efforts will be noted and appreciated. The British are notoriously bad at learning other languages in order to do business within other countries; with the advent and widespread use of the Internet, this may be an issue that is largely resolved for us as other cultures learn English in order that they may make the most of the unique advantages offered. However, you would be wise to remember that the Germans have a saying: 'We will sell to you in any language, but we will only buy from you in German'.

The next stage of observation takes place when you meet and begin to develop a relationship. Observe how people behave. Are they very formal, or very relaxed? Do they touch or avoid touching? These are all valuable insights into how to fit in with the culture.

Remember that we like people who are like ourselves. Everyone has experience, either personally or through observation, of the fact that opposites attract. Despite this, the norm is for similarities to attract. People in long-term relationships often look quite alike, too – they take the desire to see a mirror image a step further than would be the case in a friendship or business relationship. Consequently your efforts to understand and emulate another culture are likely to pay off handsomely in a business relationship.

Analyse

It is a good idea not only to know how people behave, but also why they behave in certain ways. Understanding the underlying reason for something both helps you to get it right and enhances your relationship with others. Think about someone observing our culture; things they might notice include:

- We eat fish on a Friday.
- We suffer poor service in silence.
- On meeting someone, we smile, shake hands and make eye contact.
- Despite this, we rarely make eye contact on a crowded bus or train.
- Touch can make people uncomfortable, with the exception of an expected handshake.
- Everything stops for football.

A recent radio discussion was concerned with how a settlement consultant helped American expatriates feel at home in Britain; the opening gambit of the consultant's seminar was to hold up a milk carton. The Americans immediately burst into laughter; they would never put up with such a poorly designed article and couldn't believe that the British did. For them, this one item defined the British and their culture, and also expressed the difference between that and the Americans and their culture.

Knowing what to expect guides people's behaviour. Remember also that people are often very flattered to be asked about their country's culture and traditions. Most people enjoy talking about themselves and will appreciate you showing an interest.

Act accordingly

Once you have observed and understood something, amend your own behaviour to suit and assimilate your new habits into your everyday ritual. Don't become a mimic overnight – little by little should encourage and impress. It is arguably better to show improvement in your understanding over a period of time, so demonstrating that this is a long-term commitment and something at which you are prepared to work. Once you have taken on board everything you have learned, it is time once more to observe.

By following the cycle you become, by degrees, more comfortable with the culture in which you are working. You do not need to lose your essential British ways or subsume your own personality, just act in a way that makes people more comfortable when doing business with you.

Conclusion

People like to talk about themselves and like people who are like themselves. This knowledge, if acted upon, can be a powerful asset to the global negotiator.

Do not be afraid to try speaking a few words of the language; people will appreciate your efforts and may even find it endearing if your pronunciation is less than perfect. It gives them a chance to correct you, which begins to develop a bond, and at the very least you tried.

Above all acknowledge differences, do not ignore them; after all, it would be a dull world if we were all the same.

Useful **tips**

1. Accept that different cultures have different values and behaviours.
2. Make an effort to understand alternative cultures.
3. Pick up a bit of the language.
4. Show an interest in what is happening and why.
5. Be respectful.

Chapter 8EIGHT

Using an advocate

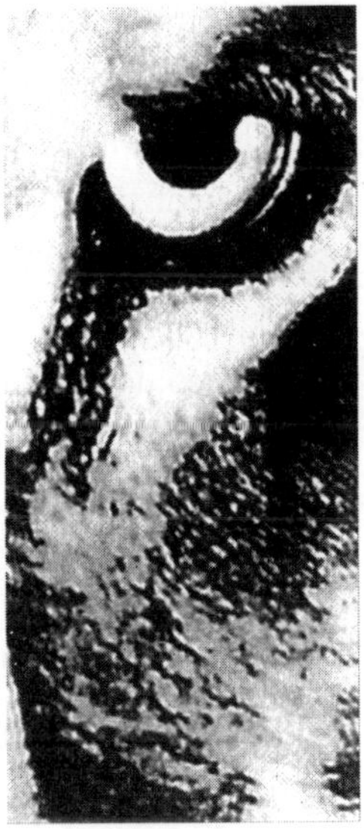

This chapter looks at the practice and process of using someone else to negotiate on your behalf.

Introduction

There are times when for whatever reason you may need to use someone to handle the negotiation process on your behalf. This may be because specialist knowledge is required, for example, in the case of a lawyer or specialist consultant. If, for example, you are looking to buy a new telecommunications system, then it is probably safe to assume that the seller knows much more than you, as the buyer, might know. Such a purchase would most likely represent a hefty expense for your company, so you would not be able to afford to make the wrong choices. You may choose to deal with this by employing a specialist to conduct negotiations on your behalf.

Times when you might require an advocate include:

- whenever legal action must be taken or responded to;
- when a company is in a great deal of debt to you or has become insolvent;
- when insurance claims must be made or met;
- when finance for the business has to be obtained; or,
- where union officials conduct wage bargaining on behalf of others.

Whilst using an advocate is an acceptable method of dealing with such issues, it is not an excuse for you to abdicate all responsibility to the expert. It will be necessary for you to take certain steps to ensure that all goes according to your plan.

These steps are:

- check out your expert to be sure that they are what they say they are;
- learn as much as possible so that you have a grasp of the technology or situation;
- set a budget;
- prepare a written statement to show what you want to achieve;
- brief your expert fully;
- follow the proceedings closely, being prepared to step in at any point should you feel it necessary; and,
- report on the outcome and review the processes undergone.

Advice or advocacy

In simple terms, the difference between advice and advocacy might be thought of as follows. With advice, you might seek the opinions of several people, weigh up what they tell you or recommend and then draw your own conclusions. You might take advice or leave it. The final decision and whatever action is deemed necessary is yours alone to take and you are entirely in control.

With advocacy, you might still take advice from a number of sources and you will certainly brief your advocate on your objectives and expectations, but then you hand things over – you are in their hands. You might also find that your objectives and expectations are considered unrealistic and that they need to be tempered in the light of your advocate's expert knowledge and experience. You still have ultimate control in that you may dismiss your advocate at any time (although possibly at a cost), but it is the advocate who acts while you watch.

It is precisely this level of power held by the advocate that makes taking the steps outlined above necessary.

Check out your expert

It is a sad fact that not everyone is as honest as they might be and so it will pay you to do some research into the credentials of your prospective advocate. Have they really worked with the multinational they claim to have on their CV? And were their results actually as impressive as stated? A couple of phone calls might be all it takes to establish credentials, but it might cost you dearly if you choose not to bother.

It is also worth considering using advisers who are at a distance, as it were, because although confidentiality ought to be guaranteed when using professionals, people do talk and they might also have a conflict of interests which they do not declare. So, if you are looking to acquire a small local company that would nicely round off your business interests, consider using a solicitor from further afield to draft up legal documents.

Learn as much as possible

Experts have power over us because of their specialist knowledge. This is something for which we pay dearly and so they often aren't too keen to make us as wise as they are. However, there is little that cannot be ascertained by conducting some research on your own. Your aim here is not to become an expert in your own right, it is to ensure that you have a sound working knowledge and an understanding of the standard terms used.

What you are doing here is taking out insurance; if you have a working knowledge, it is unlikely that experts will try to take advantage of you. The fact that you know at least a little of what they know will make them unsure of both the extent of your knowledge and their ability to pull the wool over your eyes.

Set a budget

How much are you prepared to invest in your venture? How do you know what is a realistic amount? How will you recognise a fair deal if one comes your way?

Your research into the subject will come in useful at the budget setting stage, too. You should have a grasp of what the market is running at and what you get for your money. Don't forget that you need also to budget for the cost of your expert.

Prepare a written statement

You know exactly what you want to achieve as the result of the negotiation. Make sure that everyone else on your team understands as fully as you do. Also, if you are negotiating something that will impact upon other areas of the company, get everyone involved to discuss the requirements and implications.

You should also consider and identify your BATNA – that is, Best Alternative To a Negotiated Agreement. For example, if you cannot negotiate the installation and maintenance of a new switchboard within budget, what will you do instead? BATNAs require a degree of compromise; the key is that your BATNA, should you choose to follow that option, should not require as much compromise as the best agreement that you can negotiate. Beware of falling into the trap of a deal at any cost; some deals are just too costly to accept.

Once you have set objectives and agreed a budget and a BATNA, write these up in a report and circulate it to all interested parties.

Brief your expert fully

Make sure that your expert in particular has a good grasp of what it is you are trying to achieve. If that means that you have to pay for the expert to spend a week or two in the organisation getting a feel for how things work, then bite the bullet and pay. Someone who is ill-informed will not get you the best deal available by anything other than pure chance.

Follow the proceedings closely

You have to trust your expert – up to a point. By checking out your advocate and doing your homework you have prepared the ground for success. You cannot, however, leave things up to the expert alone from now on. Make sure that you schedule regular progress meetings. Attend negotiations yourself, if that is appropriate, even if you only go along to observe the proceedings.

Should things not be progressing the way you expected or feel that they should, step in. This might be anything from halting the negotiation so that you can have a meeting with your advocate to clarify a few points, to dismissing the advocate and taking over yourself. Only you will know what is appropriate.

Report and review

In this, as in all things, we should learn from what has happened. Conduct a post mortem on proceedings and see what, if anything, you should do differently in future as a result of this latest experience. Also, prepare a report of the outcome for all interested parties and circulate it as promptly as you can. Encourage feedback if necessary.

Conclusion

There are times when using an advocate is the best course of action for you to take. Do not be dazzled, however, by claims of expertise or seemingly impressive credentials. Much of the time this is simply part of setting the stage in order to boost credibility and power.

Make sure that you are in control of the situation; after all, your expert will move on to the next contract when the time comes anyway, whereas you might not have the same luxury.

Useful **tips**

1. Check and double check credentials.
2. Set a budget.
3. Prepare a report with input from all interested parties so that you know exactly what you want to achieve.
4. Consider your BATNA.
5. Brief your expert fully – leave as little as possible to chance.
6. Keep a close eye on the proceedings.
7. Learn from the experience.

Chapter 9NINE

Dealing with conflict

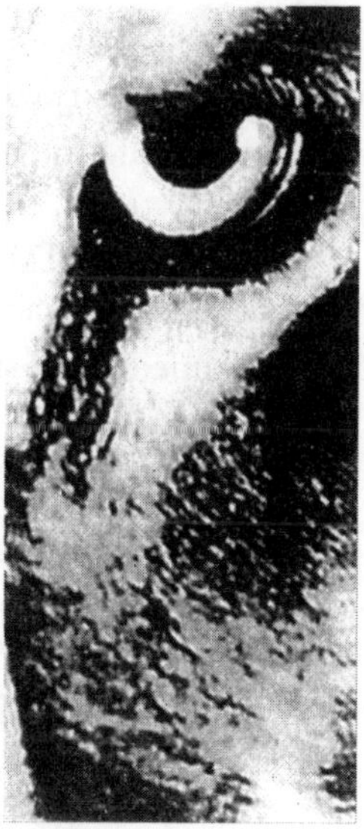

This chapter looks at the issue of conflict and how to deal with it if it arises during a negotiation.

Introduction

Within a negotiating situation, there are certain rules that relate to conflict. If the parties ignore these rules, the negotiation is likely to break down into futile argument with little result for either party.

The first rule with regard to arguments is to make sure that your position is strong and clear. It is important to be well prepared and to keep your arguments well supported and to the point. The more relevant information that you have, the more effective your argument is likely to be. Irrelevant arguments are not likely to lend you credibility and a fuzzy position will indicate weakness.

The second rule with regard to conflict is to make sure that your arguments are capable of persuading your opposite number. In order to do this, you will need as much information as possible about him.

The final rule is that you should avoid attacking or threatening your counterpart, except as an absolute last resort. Threats are rarely worth carrying through – just how much power do you really have over the other person – and you run the risk of looking silly or losing face.

Conflict

Similar rules about conflict pertain to both competitive and collaborative negotiation. Specific behaviours in collaborative negotiation would include effective communication behaviour such as actively listening, paraphrasing, sermonising and disclosing. A useful communication tactic is to label behaviour by giving advance warnings. 'I would like to ask you a question ...' or 'I feel that I need to tell you that...' Behavioural labelling slows down the negotiation process and gives both parties time to gather their thoughts and prepare responses.

Functions of conflict

Before we go on to look at somc of thc ways in which you can deal with conflict, let's try and analyse what it is that conflict does. It can be a constructive force. As a central part of everyone's life, it helps people bring to the surface issues that they would not normally talk about. It can help bring people closer together. Many people find conflict difficult to handle and destructive. However, conflict does not need to be destructive. The following chapter offers a way of identifying the two types of conflict: constructive and destructive conflict.

Constructive conflicts

These types of conflict:

- tend to be centred on interests rather than needs;
- tend to be open and dealt with openly;
- are capable of helping a relationship develop;
- focus on flexible methods for solving disputes; and,
- help both parties reach their objectives.

Destructive conflicts

These types of conflict:

- tend to be centred on people's needs rather than interests or issues of fact;
- focus on personalities, not actions or behaviours: 'You are an awkward so-and-so' rather than 'You've been awkward recently, what's been wrong?'
- involve face-saving and preservation of power;
- attack relationships;
- concentrate on 'quick fix', short-term solutions; and,
- tend to repeat themselves.

Mapping conflict

Once you've identified the nature of the conflict, you might wish to consider how it came about. Conflict doesn't just happen, it develops through clearly identifiable stages. These stages are often not identified by the parties involved. They can be labelled as follows:

1. No conflict

The first stage is, of course, no conflict at all. This stage means that there are either no differences between the parties or else one or more of the parties are afraid, for one reason or another, to express a difference. This is a stage where parties may be avoiding conflict.

2. Unexpressed conflict

This stage occurs when one party feels that there is something wrong, but will not or cannot express it. Many of us may have been in situations where we feel that there is something wrong with a relationship, but the other party refuses to identify the problem. The classic case is of the husband-wife relationship where the husband or wife asks what is wrong, only to be answered, nothing. Such unexpressed conflicts can turn into open conflict very quickly.

3. Problem identification

This stage will involve one or both parties identifying the issues that are generally interest issues that can be addressed easily at this stage. If issues are relational or emotional, however, it may be that the next stage of conflict is reached.

4. Dispute

The fourth stage is one where conflict has started to get out of hand. Parties will bring in issues that are not related to the problem. A party's needs have not been met so he or she will escalate the conflict, although there is a stage in which parties may try to involve others in the conflict, to try to obtain help.

5. Help

The fifth stage may involve other people either in an official or unofficial capacity. Individuals will appeal to a third party to attempt to resolve the conflict. Such a strategy can be dangerous for the third party, but generally their aim should be to get the parties talking again before the situation degenerates further into the penultimate stage.

6. Flight or fight

The sixth stage is one in which people tend to become very emotional and may allow the conflict to degenerate into physical or verbal aggression – hitting the other party or name calling. The conflict is such that the parties involved no longer feel safe and will be forced to leave the relationship or attempt to destroy the other party or the relationship itself.

7. The conflict cycle

The final stage can demonstrate that conflict repeats itself. Once we get into stage 6 it is very difficult to emerge. People need to feel safe when they communicate and effective communication helps them feel safe. As soon as safety is challenged, conflict can be perpetuated because we can't take the risk of talking to the other party. People in this position will often legitimise their position by talking about 'principles' or 'rights' as though the conflict is outside of themselves. Such conflicts may be impossible to handle.

Once you understand the nature of conflict and the way it has come about, the next stage is to manage it. The first stage in managing conflict is to structure and analyse the underlying issues.

Structuring the issues

When conflict takes place, individuals tend to bring unnecessary baggage. Few, if any of us, stop to analyse the issues when our partner has been caught seeing someone else or the sales manager orders some printing without clearing it through the boss. Conflict here moves quickly through the stages, with no attempt to examine the issues.

Nonetheless, if we want to manage conflict we have to consider the issues. This can be done by means of **DRIVE**.

D Data or factual issues relate to the facts about the problem. We may be in conflict because the April invoices have gone missing, which threatens our potential safety.

R Relational issues reflect the nature of the relationship. The nature of conflict about the invoices will depend on the nature of the relationship. In a weak relationship, conflict is likely to be of a longer duration.

I Interest issues impact upon what needs the parties are trying to serve and what they are trying to achieve to meet those needs.

V Value issues involve individual sets of values which dictate attitudes. Issues here are about assumptions of what is 'right' or 'wrong'.

E Emotional issues are tied to the way in which a person's individual goals and needs are met. This set of issues includes concepts such as pride, dignity and fairness.

Managing conflict

Once you've analysed and structured the issues in conflict, you can look at some of the tools you can use to manage them. Remember, though, that it helps to be as creative as possible in searching for solutions to overcome conflict. The narrower your search for information and solutions, the less successful your conflict management strategy is likely to be.

There are a number of broad strategies that may help you to manage conflict. The first of these is in the field of enquiry. Once you have structured the issues, you may need to find out why the issues have led to conflict. Enquiry can involve:

- checking by using your own words to paraphrase what the other person has said and to ask if they feel that you have understood;
- interpreting by offering your own understanding of the situation. 'I think that you are angry because... but you aren't saying so. Is that true?';
- feedback and negative feedback to give your own feelings about the person's behaviour before asking for their opinion. 'You've heard how I feel, is there anything you want to say?' Feedback can include disclosure 'I don't like to tell you this, but I am...'

The second broad strategy is control. Control involves you in stepping back from the issues that are generating the conflict and your feelings about it.

Control techniques can include relaxation exercises such as those outlined in Chapter Four on Dealing with Pressure. Other methods include 'RDA statements'.

- Resent.
- Demand.
- Appreciate.

Thus you might say to your partner:

- 'I resent the fact that you didn't wash the pots last night.'
- 'I demand that you do your share of the housework.'
- 'I appreciate the fact that you cleaned the bathroom last week.'

This helps to develop the elements of a contract for future behaviour. RDA statements should concentrate on past behaviour. That is, what the difficult person does or says, and not what you consider that person to be.

A variant of RDA statements is the 4R series. Using this model you:

- **Receive** the other person's comments without interrupting. This shows that you are listening and value the other person's statement.
- **Repeat** the other person's comments as objectively as possible. This can help the other person open up about the problem.
- **Request** the other person's proposed way of dealing with the problem. People who are unable to deal with conflict are often unable to offer solutions, instead releasing tension and wanting to talk about the problem.
- **Review** the possible options. The final strategy is assertiveness. Assertiveness training became very popular in the late 1980s, and can be a useful way of communicating in the context of a good relationship. Assertiveness is about honestly disclosing your feelings in a way which is acceptable to the other person in the relationship.

Assertion techniques include 'broken record'. This involves you in repeating your statement using the same tone of voice and volume. 'I appreciate you are busy but…' and briefly stating what you need or want, your belief or opinion. Assertiveness is really only honesty or congruence in communication.

Conclusion

Whatever method you use dealing with conflict or potential conflict involves you attempting to restore effective communication as soon as possible. Because conflict can involve emotional, value, interest and relational issues our reaction is often dictated by our primitive behaviour patterns. Our initial reaction is to run away or turn and fight. In order to deal with these reactions we need to step outside the issues and to manage ourselves. Without managing our 'self' we are immediately discarding half of the resources within the relationship which we need to manage.

Useful **tips**

1. Negotiation goes on constantly.
2. Negotiation is about power in relationships.
3. Negotiation can break down into conflict.
4. In dealing with conflict, 'self' is very important.
5. It is possible to identify two types of conflict, constructive and destructive.
6. Managing conflict involves recognition of conflict and structuring the issues to resume communication.
7. There are a number of techniques that you can use to do this including DRIVE, RDA statements and 4R responses.

Chapter 10TEN

Assertiveness skills

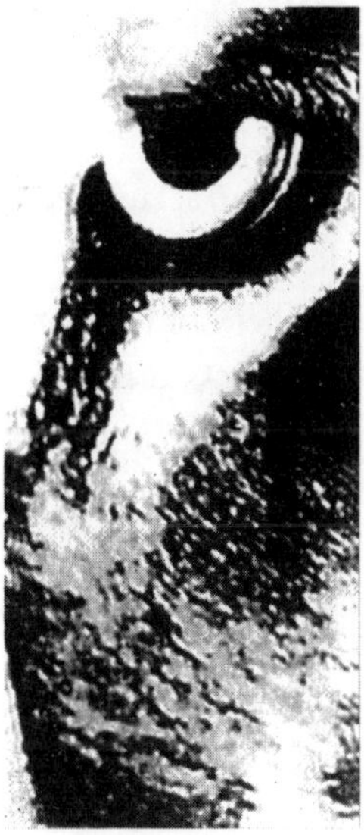

It helps to be assertive if you want to be a good negotiator. This chapter concentrates on how assertiveness skills can be used to improve your working relations.

Introduction

Assertiveness is about reducing and managing conflict, not about creating it. The most difficult part of management can be dealing with people – they can act unpredictably especially in times of stress or disagreement. Managers who assert themselves effectively with employees, colleagues, suppliers and customers, will get better results, save time and be less stressed. Assertiveness helps to provide solutions to difficult situations and to reach constructive compromises that suit everyone. Knowing how to do this well is an important management skill.

What is assertiveness?

Assertiveness is about honestly expressing feelings and needs. Assertiveness allows people to relate to one another in an open and frank way, whilst respecting each other's views and opinions. The aim is to get relationships out of the emotive modes of aggression and passivity, onto a rational level, focusing discussion on the problem, not on the personalities involved. Constructive solutions can then be found which take account of everyone's needs and wants.

Assertiveness is not to be confused with aggression. Aggressive behaviour ignores the feelings and opinions of others and violates their rights. Aggression may seem to release tension, induce a sense of power, solve problems quickly and earn the respect of others. In the long-term it creates an atmosphere of tension and resentment. If staff feel intimidated, they are less effective, withhold information, become demoralised and in some cases, may even leave.

Passive or 'non-assertive' behaviour is not standing up for yourself or expressing your views inadequately, if at all. Conflict is avoided, decisions are delayed, self-esteem is low, there is frustration and loss of respect from colleagues. Passivity results from being afraid of the consequences of getting into trouble. Passive people often think they are just being polite or helpful.

Why be assertive?

Handling conflict

Assertiveness helps to defuse difficult situations where people are angry or upset. Conflicts can be resolved and effective solutions found.

Staff development

Assertive relations with staff take account of their feelings and views. This helps them work more effectively, and encourages them to make a greater contribution in terms of new ideas and improvements to current practices.

Customer relations

Dealing assertively with customers, especially during negotiations, involves being honest about what can be achieved and not making promises that can't be kept.

Communications and teamwork

When everyone in an organisation feels comfortable about expressing their views, communication is improved and people are more likely to say what they really think. Everyone is more aware of where problems lie, and is happier about suggesting solutions and working together to implement them.

Confidence

Assertive people are more decisive. Knowing that a situation was handled well improves confidence. Worry and stress are reduced and more gets done. Time management improves. Staff are happier working for someone who is comfortable in a leadership role, and this also affects the attitude of suppliers, bankers, etc.

Negotiating skills

Being assertive and confident helps people to get better outcomes from negotiations of all kinds.

Rights and responsibilities

When people are intimidated or bullied, they often feel that their feelings do not matter, that they are getting things out of proportion and deserve to be pushed around. The concept of rights enables someone to judge whether they are being fairly treated, and gives them the confidence to take the appropriate action. Rights are defined as 'something to which you are entitled'. Everybody has certain basic rights. Here is a suggested list:

- The right to say what you really think.
- The right to a fair hearing.
- The right to be different, to be an individual.
- The right to be treated with respect (eg, to be asked, not told).
- The right to say 'no'.
- The right to make mistakes.

If rights are fully accepted, then it will be easier to defend them. With rights come responsibilities, for example, people have the right occasionally to make mistakes – but there is also a responsibility to acknowledge it and to take action. You are also responsible for respecting the rights of others.

Assertive thinking

Positive mental attitude

Many people are defeated before they start because they don't believe that they can succeed. This affects the way they use assertiveness methods, and influences the way they behave when trying to apply them. If you believe you can't do something, you won't. If you believe you can, you probably will – and even if you don't get it completely right, you will probably achieve at least some of your objectives. Beliefs affect behaviour. Whilst you can't change things overnight, getting into the habit of thinking positively about future outcomes will improve your confidence. To make assertiveness work you must believe that you can be assertive and that others are prepared to relate to you on that basis.

Anticipation

For assertiveness to be effective it is important to plan carefully what you want to say beforehand. It is particularly important to be positive immediately before dealing with difficult situations. Take a deep breath, imagine yourself dealing with the situation well and responding assertively. Have confidence in your method. This will improve your performance.

Assertive communication

The aim of assertive communication is to negotiate and agree a solution that is acceptable to all involved. This can be achieved by a simple three stage process:

- Hear and acknowledge the other person's point of view (eg, 'I understand that this new deadline is important').
- State your own views, feelings and opinions (eg, 'However, I already have other important tasks to complete at the same time').
- Agree a way forward that is acceptable to both parties (eg, 'Why don't we contact the customers involved, explain the situation and find out which work must be done immediately? We can then prioritise the workload and perhaps get some extra help if needed.').

Further assertiveness techniques

Saying '**no**'

Many passive people are afraid to say 'no'. However, if you cannot possibly do something it is much better to be honest and say so, rather than being polite. This can stop tensions developing and help focus on finding effective solutions.

Empathising

Empathy is when you put yourself in someone else's shoes. Combine empathy with stating your needs. For example, 'I know you're really busy at the moment, but…'.

Clarification

This is used when you think that what was agreed and what is currently happening are different. For example, 'I understood we were going to do it this way, but now I think you want it done that way; am I correct?' You may want to clarify a task or role assigned. If the discrepancy is deliberate, being assertive will have confirmed that the agreement originally made still stands, or that circumstances have changed – either way, doubt has been removed.

Stating the consequences

This should only be used as a last resort. This approach warns people of the consequences, but also gives options for the behaviour to change (eg, 'If this happens again, I will have to apply the formal disciplinary procedure.') Consequence assertion must only be used when you are prepared to use the appropriate sanctions.

Asking questions

The aim is to discover the other person's wants and needs by asking clear and direct questions, such as, 'Is this the only problem you are having?', or 'So, are you telling me that the new system is in fact giving you more work?'. It is useful when people are being indirect. You can find out exactly where they stand. It can be used to establish whether a certain action is acceptable, to collect information and to check if the other person has the same understanding. It encourages others to express themselves assertively.

Repetition

When negotiating or in discussion, repetition can be very effective. Do not simply repeat your point – this will be dull. Restating your case, in different ways, ensures that your point is made and that the other person has listened and understood it.

Putting assertiveness into practice

Using assertiveness to deal with conflict

If you can maintain a calm, assertive approach when faced with aggression, the other person usually calms down and behaves more rationally. Do not deal with really difficult situations at once. Arrange a later meeting so that everyone can calm down, and you have time to consider what you will say. There are several methods for dealing with aggression. A very effective way is to agree with people who are angry, for example saying 'Yes, I can see that you are very upset about this'. You have not conceded anything, but have acknowledged their feelings. This should slow them down, and should allow you to go on to explain your views calmly. It is also useful when you are pounced on by an aggrieved person to ask clear and direct questions. Instead of reacting defensively, asking questions gives you information, time to think, time for the other person to calm down and prevents you from taking a hurried decision.

Leadership

Respect the rights of employees, and encourage them to be assertive too. At the same time, employees expect leadership. It is important to be able to assert your authority with confidence. If one person is allowed to get away with things, or to push someone around, others will become demoralised and even disruptive. Surprisingly, you also have to be firm if you wish to praise an employee without embarrassment. Giving employees constructive feedback based on facts and evidence, rather than opinions and qualitative judgements, is easier if employees are treated assertively. Assertive teams communicate and work together more effectively and rationally, and will be able to resolve conflicts quickly and satisfactorily.

Stress

Calmness is crucial. It cools things down and helps you think rationally. Much conflict results from a build up of stress and is often a way to let off steam. Assert yourself when people are less likely to be under stress. Do not react immediately if things are getting on top of you. Give yourself a cooling off period. Finally, before you assert yourself, take a deep breath and try to relax; this will help you think and act more rationally.

Conclusion

There is no mileage in being a doormat any more than there is in being an ogre. Choosing instead to behave assertively – and remember that we do choose our behaviour – gives you a third option that need not involve fight or flight. In addition those who behave assertively generally command more respect and are taken more seriously in business.

Useful **tips**

1. Assertiveness methods are not suitable for every situation and some conflicts can't be avoided.
2. Be natural. It takes time to learn about assertiveness and how to use it. Incorporate assertiveness techniques into your management style and do not expect your behaviour to change overnight.
3. Don't be put off by failure. Take a long-term view, stay positive and learn from your mistakes.
4. Attend an assertiveness training course.

Part 3THREE

Negotiation in practice

Chapter 11 ELEVEN

Tendering for contracts

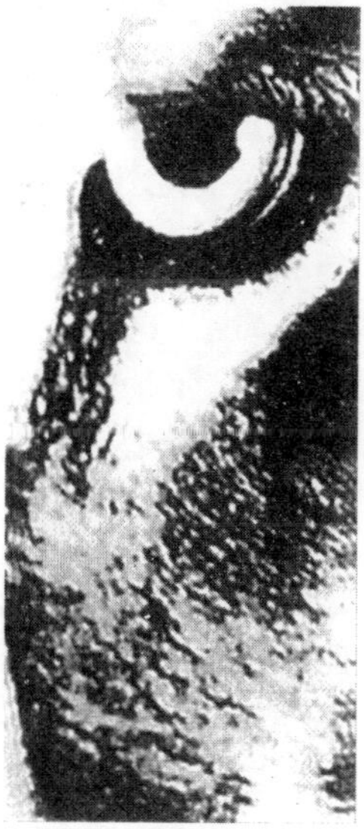

One of the most important negotiations into which you will ever enter is when you are tendering for a contract. Sometimes you will only get as far as making a written submission; sometimes you may have the opportunity to make a formal presentation; and sometimes you will need to negotiate the final agreement. This chapter looks at the process of tendering for contracts and outlines how it may be approached.

Introduction

Winning a major contract can transform the fortunes of a small business. Many businesses depend entirely upon three or four major contracts. The introduction of Compulsory Competitive Tendering (CCT) significantly increased the amount of public sector work being put out to tender. The government hopes that CCT will increase cost efficiency within the public sector and provide work for the private sector.

The importance of tendering is growing as many organisations replace permanent labour with specialists employed on a more short-term basis. Tendering is most commonly associated with the construction industry, but is increasingly used in a wide range of businesses. Knowing how to tender for contracts is vital – you also need to know how to find contracts that are open for tender. There are some basic principles that can be applied generally.

Selection procedures differ within and between industries, ranging from the submission of basic quotes to a more complex series of interviews and presentations. To give yourself the best chance of winning you need to understand and comply with the process adopted by the customer. Smaller contracts often have less formal procedures – but they should be taken no less seriously.

What is tendering?

Tendering is the process by which work for a set period or project is publicly advertised (in the press or by correspondence), allowing competing firms to bid for that work. Having received quotes or applications from interested companies, the client selects the preferred contractor and a detailed contract is agreed. The basic contractual terms may form part of the tender document.

Cost, quality and time are the most significant issues in tendering. While one may be of higher importance in a particular contract, they form a connected package – each affecting the others. Assessing your chances of success (your competitiveness) involves examining what you provide and its value for money.

Preparing tenders for larger contracts takes a lot of work – it can be costly if a series of them prove to be unrewarding.

Identifying contracts

Invitations to tender may be made through public announcement or by direct invitation.

Under European legislation all public sector contracts above set values must be put out to tender throughout the European Union. These are advertised through Supplement 'S' of the *Official Journal of the European Communities*, and through other sources including *TED* (*Tenders Electronic Daily*, the on-line version of the Official Journal) and the Euro-Information Service. Most UK government departments have publications in which contracts are advertised, eg *MOD Contracts Bulletin* or *MOD Works Services Opportunities*. Information should be readily available from departments that interest you.

Invitations to tender for private sector contracts are often advertised in trade magazines and the local press. Your trade association should be able to advise you and journals are often available through your local library.

To issue a direct invitation to tender, potential clients must be aware of your firm's existence. You can initiate contact by registering interest. Although large public sector contracts must be advertised, a vast number of lower-value projects need not be. These are awarded through local and regional offices of the relevant department; it can be worthwhile approaching these on your own initiative. Potential suppliers undergo a thorough assessment before inclusion on the appropriate list of companies. It can also lead to referral to other departments. For private work it is worth contacting potential customers and keeping them informed of your services. This can be done initially via a mail-shot, but try to establish a relationship with a contact person within that company.

You may also spot contracts that are too large for your firm to bid for directly. The company that gains the contract may need to sub-contract some of the work. Details of who has won a contract may be worth finding and chasing, eg, through trade or local press.

Identifying customer requirements

As with job applications or interviews, you should obtain as much information as you can before preparing your tender. The first information you should look at is the advert or invitation itself. This should outline the job and is worth examining in detail. Further information can then be requested from the client. Do not hesitate to ask for details; by helping, the company helps itself to find the right supplier. Use any contacts that you have within the organisation.

Make sure that you understand exactly what the customer wants, and that you can deliver it, before going too far. Many companies work to recognised quality standards; they may require their suppliers to meet those standards too. Standards such as ISO9000 are not compulsory, but are now so widespread as to be expected. Alongside references, these represent your professional competence to the client.

Developing a package

Producing a detailed tender involves considerable time and resources, so needs careful consideration before you begin. Consider the following:

- Current workload, and the availability of labour, equipment, materials, etc.
- The effect of new jobs on your cash flow and capital.
- The type, size, value and location of the new job – if it differs from your regular method of working is it appropriate to pursue it?
- Previous knowledge of the client and other parties involved (eg, architect, sub-contractors).
- Terms and conditions of the contract (eg, fixed price, allocation of liability). The degree of responsibility taken on affects your financial commitment to a contract.
- Degree of competition (are you in with a chance?).
- Market conditions prevailing.
- Time allowed and available to prepare a tender.
- Working with subcontractors.

The contract holder often has to organise sub-contractors. Their quotes will be required before you can submit a final estimate. At times you will be required to work alongside sub-contractors chosen by the client. The Construction (Design and Management) Regulations 1994 require main contract holders to organise and oversee a safety policy covering all those involved on the site. For all types of work, it is important to ensure that arrangements with sub-contractors support those you have made with the client.

Identifying a price

Pricing must be realistic. Estimates or quotes are important in a successful bid, but price alone rarely determines the outcome. Competition makes factors like quality count. If you add value to a product (eg, by increasing quality or adding services) you should be able to charge a premium (if the added value is worth something to the customer).

It is important to include as many details as possible in the original quote to avoid disputes later. For contracts based on intellectual or creative services, clarify the way payment affects rights to the ideas, artwork, etc – at each stage of the contract. Your price should provide enough profit margin to make the contract worth doing. Building contractors have had difficulty passing on recent rises in overheads (eg, health and safety costs) to the client.

Assembling a tender document

Time allowed to prepare a tender can vary tremendously. Often clients do not provide enough time for preparation. Do not be afraid to ask for an extension, others probably feel the same way. If the client already has a specific idea of what the work should entail the details should be carefully checked before any contract is entered into.

Government departments often issue standard forms in response to applications from private businesses. Contact the relevant department to confirm procedures. In the final stages of the process they may ask for financial and management records as well as references. Both local authorities and private companies may issue questionnaires. These are quite detailed, covering, for example, insurance details, previous work, equipment available to you, ownership details, association membership and references, number of employees and the complete range of services that your business offers.

When your initial application has been accepted you should receive a series of documents from the client (or someone acting on their behalf). These may include plans or drawings to date and the official 'form of tender'. Labour rates and cost control systems may be detailed as part of a tender. Before you sign the final form, check every detail.

Presenting and negotiating

Raise any areas of concern as soon as possible, to avoid serious problems once work has got underway. The way you present them will depend upon the job itself, but it is common for the client or their representative to visit you before the final choice is made. It is important to find out what is expected of you in advance – it may have a bearing on your decision to allocate resources to the tender. You may have to 'pitch' yourself to a board of interviewers, or submit a sample of your work to be examined; check whether payment is made for this.

You may have to negotiate the price or details of the contract. Methods of cost control will probably have been set down earlier, and may have to be justified or explained. It is worth investigating the standard agreements within your industry.

Legal factors

Contract law is complex; seek advice from a solicitor and familiarise yourself with the chapters that apply to your business. Be aware of your responsibilities under public liability and health and safety law. This is particularly relevant to construction sites – stringent regulations have been introduced affecting all contractors within the industry. You should have insurance appropriate to your industry, to cover public or product liability, etc.

Several EC Directives, introduced into Britain as statutory instruments, cover tendering within the EU. These include: Supplies Directive, Works Directive, Services Directive and Utilities Directive. 'Compliance' and 'Remedies' make provisions for the protection of the tenderer. The World Trade Organisation (WTO) Government Procurement Agreement (GPA) is an international agreement covering the procurement of supplies by certain bodies, and provides for the debriefing of unsuccessful tenderers upon request.

Contract disputes

Breach of contract may constitute an actual or anticipatory breach. Actual breach occurs when one party fails to perform their duties and may enable repudiation of the contract; alternatively, the other party may simply wish to claim for damages. Anticipatory breach occurs where one party states that they do not intend to carry out a particular part of their contract or puts themselves in such a position as to make them unable to carry out the task.

There are so many aspects relating to contracts, their formation, implications and results that it would arguably be unreasonable to expect all parties to understand everything. It is essential, however, that you understand at least the most basic concepts and have access to some aid should any problems occur. If you are in any doubt about where you stand in a dispute with a customer or supplier, you would be well advised to consult a solicitor.

Conclusion

If you are planning to tender for contracts, prepare your bid carefully. Try to charge a realistic price and not to bid for work that, however tempting, would leave the company overstretched. Remember that your presentation is key: it is the first step in the process of negotiating the contract and a marvellous opportunity to make a positive impression.

Useful **tips**

1. Only tender for what you can realistically deliver. Letting a client down could prove costly to your professional reputation and finances.

2. Obtain information specific to your own industry and particular client groups (eg, Government bodies) before taking any action.

3. Take time and effort to prepare a quality presentation, which takes account of typical codes of practice within your industry, including processes, estimating, etc.

4. The possession of recognised quality standards is increasingly vital if you are to compete effectively at the tender stage.

5. References from previous clients will greatly improve your application.

6. If you win a high proportion of the contracts for which you tender, you may be charging less than you could.

Chapter 12 TWELVE

Staff relations

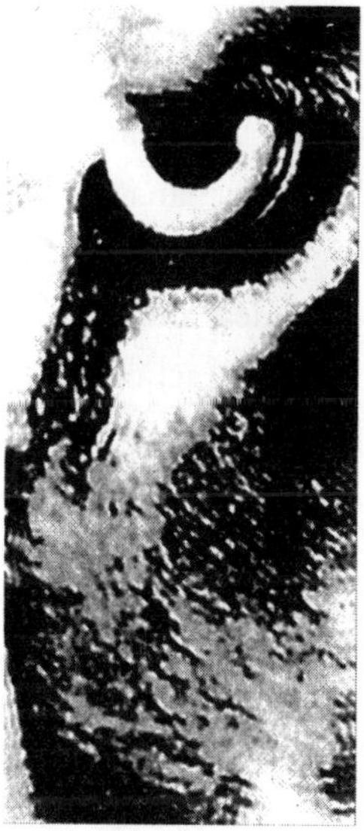

Once you employ staff, you will certainly find yourself regularly negotiating with them. This chapter describes ways to develop good relations with employees and, in particular, how to approach relations with trade unions.

Introduction

No business can operate effectively if there is distrust and hostility between managers and staff. Friendly and open relations encourage higher levels of motivation, and should encourage staff to contribute their ideas and observations about how the operation can be improved. Industrial action can be disastrous for a small business. Good employee relations should ensure that disputes can be resolved quickly so that minimal damage is caused.

'Employee relations', or 'industrial relations', may be defined as the rules, practices and conventions governing the relationships between management and workforce. The term 'industrial relations' conjures up a more traditional picture of unionised heavy industry. The smaller business is better placed to establish good employee relations. Everyone can be on first name terms. Many problems can be resolved on a one to one basis. Small firms can react quickly to employee grievances and changing conditions. It is important for the owner/manager of a small business to make best use of such opportunities.

Employee representation

Ideally a small business may be seen as a group of people working together with the common goal of making the business successful. In reality, however, a business must impose at least some measure of control and discipline upon its staff, while employees may feel that they need some way to have their own collective interests represented to balance the power of management. Historically, trade unions grew up to take on this role of representing the interests of the workforce. Trade unions developed most powerfully in the large industries, negotiating improved pay and conditions for large workforces in a heavily politicised environment. In the more informal world of the small business, introducing union practices can seem like an unnecessary complication. Communication on terms and conditions has to go through the union. Discretionary pay increases based on merit may be hard to implement. Management decisions can be challenged and negotiations may take up an increasing amount of time. Overall, the prized flexibility of the small business may be diminished. Most employers now recognise that fair pay and conditions and fair management are important for business success and actively pursue ways to promote good relations with staff.

Trade unions

It is unlawful to make employment or the provision of services conditional upon union membership or non-membership. Employees normally join unions because they wish to improve their working conditions, usually because the union structure guarantees them a spokesperson. If you are approached to recognise a union or hear talk of such moves, review your own approach to employee relations. Research suggests that certain subjects of dissatisfaction including wages, promotion prospects and job security, are often linked with pressure to unionise. Dissatisfaction with the job itself is not usually an issue. You do not have to recognise a union, but it may be prudent to do so if your employees wish it. You may prefer to negotiate your own alternative consultation procedures. Refusal to recognise a union, or to come up with a suitable alternative, may cause lasting damage to relations with your staff.

Consider the number of unions you recognise. A single union simplifies negotiations but has greater power. You can restrict the number of terms and conditions that the union can negotiate. This leaves you with discretion to arrange non-negotiable items directly with the employees concerned. Consider insisting on a no-strike agreement with the union or that external arbitration will be sought before a strike is called. You may agree that all employees will be required to join the recognised union or unions – a closed shop agreement. Any closed shop agreement must comply with current legislation.

If you are managing your employee relations well, your employees are unlikely to seek union membership. If the subject does come up try to take a positive approach. Create opportunities for the issue to be openly discussed by all staff. Speak to them individually. Is everyone behind membership? Have they thought through all the pros and cons? If the workforce still wish to proceed, work positively with union representatives. Ensure that representatives are from within the business. Do whatever you can to create the right environment for negotiation by making union links part of your own measures to maintain good employee relations.

Employee representatives

Irrespective of whether unions play a role, many employers see it as good practice to appoint an employee to represent the interests of staff to the management. Consider allowing a staff representative to sit in on board meetings and be involved in senior management meetings. The workforce could select the person concerned. Representatives may be changed on a regular basis. If representatives (union or otherwise) have a good understanding of the needs of the business this should (hopefully) lead to a more responsible attitude if they are involved in negotiating pay and conditions.

Consultation

Consultation before major changes is vital. People tend to be unsettled by change, especially if it is sudden and unexpected. More importantly, they may know of factors that would have affected decisions on the measures implemented. Consultation can be simple, informal discussions. If a decision has been made, eg, a new staff appointment, let everyone know about it before it is implemented, eg, before the person starts. More involved topics may require formal meetings with relevant representatives and the circulation of consultation papers.

Important areas for consultation include working procedures and practices, changes in responsibilities, pay and conditions, major developments in the business (eg, change of ownership, acquisitions, etc) and practical changes, eg, building alterations, new seating arrangements, etc.

Communication

A great deal of suspicion and distrust can be avoided by keeping staff informed. If people feel that they do not know what is going on, they may assume there is something to hide. Information makes people feel secure and more involved in a firm's affairs.

Verbal

In the small firm, there is no substitute for talking regularly on a one-to-one basis with staff. People do not always read written circulars. One-to-one, you can make information relevant and gauge understanding. This may happen naturally in the course of work, but you may need to arrange to see those who cross your path less often. Confidentiality is important, but try to avoid keeping unnecessary secrets. Avoid having only a select few 'in the know'. Also, remember to listen. Find out what others need to know and have to say.

Meetings

Meetings, formal or informal, are a valuable communication tool. Small firms can hold meetings of all staff, larger firms may need to organise sub-groups or even a cascade briefing system. For major announcements a meeting of all staff is usually best. Meetings for particular purposes, eg, quality circles, can be used to collect feedback. If some people show little interest at meetings, do not give up and accuse everyone of apathy. Is there an underlying problem? Find ways to get them more involved.

Written communication

Noticeboards can be useful if well located, kept clutter-free, and notices are removed when out-of-date. Memos and circulars are a means of directing information to specific people and are especially useful when you need to know that information has been circulated. Do not use these officiously. A common mistake is to circulate a note to all staff when you really need to speak to particular people. Consultation papers and reports are good for informing people in more depth – as well as for seeking feedback. Ensure that the people you circulate written information to are really interested. Consider producing a simple newsletter as a way to keep everyone informed and involved. Employee handbooks are useful for updating staff on policies, procedures and activities; particularly as part of a quality control system.

Arbitration

From time to time, it maybe helpful to seek advice from the Advisory, Conciliation and Arbitration Service (ACAS) or to involve them in a dispute. In addition, they publish guidelines for employee representation in small businesses, which you may find helpful.

> Establish simple written negotiating procedures, such as: employee representative to discuss the issue with relevant manager; if agreement is not reached, representative meets managing director; if agreement is not reached, conciliation or arbitration may be sought.
>
> Establish clear bargaining arrangements, such as when and how meetings are arranged, who attends and who conducts negotiations, facilities available to representatives, time allowed for

trade union or employee group meetings, and procedures for informing staff of agreements or disputes.

- Which issues are negotiable, and which non-negotiable, should be clearly understood by all parties from the outset.
- If agreement cannot be reached, one or both sides may request the conciliation services of ACAS. If there is still no agreement, ACAS can appoint an independent arbitrator, provided both sides agree to respect the arbitrator's decision.

Reviewing employee relations

If you feel that your business has grown too big for the informal approach, review the way you relate to your employees and assess the need for more planning and formalisation. Look at the various areas of your activities that affect employee relations. It helps if you can put your approach in writing, especially where you wish to consult on a proposed policy. The text may become part of your personnel policy document. In particular, ensure that you have suitable grievance and disciplinary procedures in place.

Conclusion

The key skill when handling employee relations is, arguably, communication. If you are open and honest in your dealings and conduct your negotiations from a collaborative rather than a competitive standpoint, your chances of success and of enjoying a harmonious relationship with your staff and their representatives are greatly enhanced.

Useful **tips**

1. It is crucial to stay in touch with your staff and talk to them regularly, formally and informally. It is all too easy to cut yourself off in a separate office and to blame everything that goes wrong on troublemakers. If necessary, seek training in employee relations skills.

2. Establish orderly procedures for collective bargaining and settling disputes. Develop clear, comprehensive and consistent employment policies on recruitment, promotion, training, redundancy, etc.

3. Avoid giving favoured employees special privileges or opportunities that are not available to others.

4. Under the Social Chapter, legislation will be introduced in the European Community aimed at enforcing certain minimum standards for informing, consulting and involving employees and their representatives.

Chapter 13 THIRTEEN

Industrial tribunals

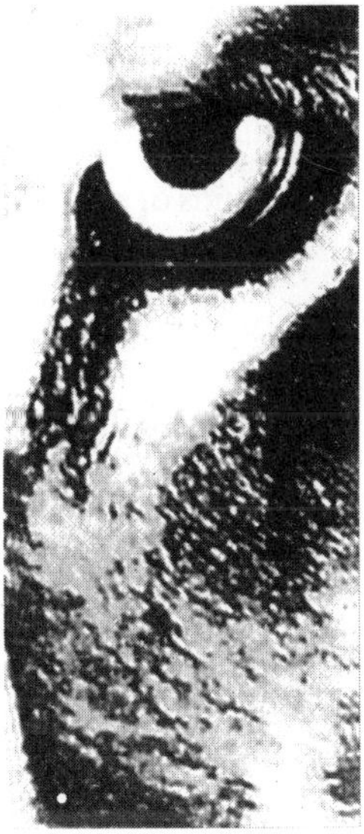

This chapter looks at industrial tribunal proceedings from an employer's viewpoint.

Introduction

Industrial tribunals are independent judicial bodies that hear cases of dispute over employment rights. They can deal with appeals about, for example, unfair dismissal, equal pay, maternity rights, discrimination on grounds of sex, disability, race, trade union membership rights, etc.

What happens at a tribunal?

Each tribunal has three members: a legally qualified chairman and two others drawn from panels – one representing employer associations, the other representing trade unions. The Chairman may sit alone in certain cases. In race discrimination cases one of the lay members normally has specialist knowledge.

Persons bringing a case to a tribunal are known as applicants; those against whom cases are brought are known as respondents. Applicants are usually employees or ex-employees; respondents are usually employers. You can represent yourself or be represented by someone else (eg, a solicitor). The procedure makes self representation straight-forward, but if in doubt seek professional advice. You will normally be responsible for the cost of your own representation.

Initial procedures

You will receive a copy of the employee's tribunal application stating their case against you, along with a copy of the booklet 'What to do if taken to an Industrial Tribunal'. Fill in and return the form that comes with this information or write to the tribunal service disputing or agreeing with the claim. This is called 'entering an appearance'. Any such statement you make is very important. If it later proves inaccurate or untruthful you can lose the case. Failure to enter an appearance means loss of entitlement to defend your case in tribunal proceedings, though you may still be required to attend as a witness. Ensure your 'appearance' reaches the tribunal within 21 days of receipt of the form. Quote the case number in this and all subsequent communication. If you are delayed in replying, inform the tribunal – they may still allow you to defend your case. The tribunal will send a copy of your 'appearance' to the applicant and another copy to ACAS (the Advisory Conciliation and Arbitration Service).

Where an employee appeals to a tribunal for breach of contract, the employer may counter claim for breach of contract. This must be within six weeks of receiving the initial application. You may need professional advice in such a case.

The role of ACAS

(Advisory Conciliation and Arbitration Service)

A settlement might be reached before the case comes to a hearing. ACAS will contact both you and the applicant and offer help to resolve the dispute. ACAS is an independent organisation giving impartial and confidential advice. ACAS cannot express judgements on the outcome of the case, assist the individual parties with their case or intervene if both parties reach an agreement of their own. However, using ACAS as an intermediary to get people talking might allow or enable you to negotiate a settlement. If an agreement has been reached, the tribunal is unlikely to hear the original case. Copies of the agreement are sent to both parties and the tribunal. Each side should also notify the tribunal when an agreement has been reached, so the case can be withdrawn.

General issues

- You can request further information if you feel that the applicant's complaint is unclear. If they refuse unreasonably, the tribunal can order them to provide the information.
- Ensure that you have copies of all documents to be used by the applicant and give them copies of those you will be using. Tribunals can make orders for witnesses to attend or for documents or further particulars to be presented.
- You will be notified of the hearing date at least 14 days in advance. If you cannot attend, write to the tribunal board immediately – state why you cannot attend and include proof of the reason. Also notify them of any other days when you cannot attend. You must ask for postponement within 14 days of being notified of the hearing date. If it is refused, you may appeal to the Employment Appeal Tribunal immediately.
- You can either send details of witness statements to the applicant and the tribunal at least a week before the hearing, or have the witness attend. Try to provide witnesses on the day of the hearing – this carries more weight. If a witness cannot attend, request a postponement. If a witness refuses to attend, write to the tribunal stating why that witness is required; the tribunal may order them to attend.

Preparing for the tribunal

As with any form of negotiation, you should prepare thoroughly. You should seek advice from ACAS, your solicitor, and other professional advisers depending upon the claim against you. The Citizen's Advice Bureau, the Equal Opportunities Commission or the Commission for Racial Equality may also be suitable contacts. Also, do not forget to check out your network for potential useful contacts.

You may need legal advice if the case rests on points of law. To argue points of fact, you will need witnesses and/or documentary evidence to support your case. Make sure all relevant documents are readily available; you will need five copies with pages numbered – three for the tribunal, one for the other side and one for the witness table. Documentation may include: contract of employment, letter of appointment, memos, wages bills, letters from customers, etc.

Before attending the hearing, make sure that your witnesses know where and when the hearing will be held. If you write out your evidence and provide copies for the tribunal you will make it easier for them to follow what you say.

Types of hearing

Although cases often go straight to the main hearing, other types of hearing might be held.

Interlocutory hearing

A hearing for the tribunal to clarify various issues or decide what orders need to be made. Such hearings don't usually include evidence.

Pre-hearing review

These may be called for by either party or the tribunal if it seems that either party's case has little chance of success. The review tribunal considers the application and notice of appearance in detail – no evidence is taken but each side can advance its argument. After assessment, the tribunal will say if it thinks a case is unlikely to succeed. A party with a weak case will be advised against continuing. If that party still wishes to continue, they will be warned that if they lose they may be liable for the other party's costs when the main hearing tribunal (which will have different members) makes its judgement. They could be required to pay a deposit as a condition of continuing. The pre-hearing tribunal's views will not be made known to the main tribunal until after it has made its judgement.

Preliminary hearing

These hearings are held if the tribunal thinks it may not have the necessary powers to deal with all aspects of the case.

Interim relief hearing

These are held when an applicant claims interim relief. The hearing chairman will decide whether the applicant is likely to succeed at the main hearing – if so, a re-employment order or an order continuing the contract of employment will be issued.

The main hearing

The tribunal decides whether the applicant's claim succeeds or fails at this hearing.

Review hearing

Review hearings are possible in certain situations, eg, on a point of law or in light of new evidence. You cannot request a review just because you disagree with the decision. Appeals are made to the Employment Appeal Tribunal – particulars are sent with a tribunal's decision. Professional legal advice is essential when appealing.

Hearing procedures

The procedure for hearings is informal and flexible. Each party may give evidence, call witnesses, and question their own or the other party's witnesses. Tribunal members can ask parties or witnesses questions. Generally, as in unfair dismissal cases, the employer gives evidence first, but the tribunal will change the order for giving evidence where appropriate. The sequence is often as follows:

> Witnesses for one side are examined, cross-examined and questioned by tribunal members.

- The process is repeated for the other side.
- Both sides sum up; whoever presented their case first gets the last word.

A typical unfair dismissal case involves three or four witnesses per side and takes a full day to hear. The process can be arduous because of its adversarial nature. Private grievances and hostility can emerge. There will always be winners and losers. The best advice is to remain calm.

Hearings are open to the press and public unless the tribunal says otherwise. The ability to have a private hearing is strictly limited. Witnesses are usually present throughout a hearing. The tribunal's clerk will explain procedures before the case starts and the tribunal will provide guidance as the hearing progresses. If you are not represented at a hearing, the case can be decided in your absence. In certain cases involving union membership issues, a trade union can be required to become a party to the proceedings.

Tribunal decisions

The decision, and reasons for it, may be announced at close of hearing The decision is always confirmed in writing later. In most cases, a summary of the reasons is provided, with extended reasons available on request within 21 days.

- Compensation – the written decision will detail any award of compensation and how it was calculated.
- The tribunal will send details to an employer required to reimburse the government for money it has paid to a successful applicant.

Interest on compensation awarded becomes payable if a successful applicant is not paid promptly. This means within 14 days of being notified in discrimination cases or within 42 days for all other cases.

Conclusion

Prepare thoroughly for the tribunal and make sure that your advocate, if you are using one, is thoroughly briefed. Remember that even if you are using a representative to negotiate on your behalf, you must accept ownership and retain control of the proceedings. Also, irrespective of the outcome and your own feelings about it, be sure to abide by the instructions and decision of the tribunal.

Useful **tips**

1. All dealings with a tribunal must be completely truthful – these are legal proceedings.

2. Consider carefully whether a case is worth contesting. Seek advice (that is what pre-hearing assessments are for). You may save money, time and anguish by negotiating a settlement without a tribunal.

3. Always reply to tribunal correspondence within the time limits specified. Notify the tribunal if there is good reason for delay. They can extend deadlines. Copy any correspondence with the tribunal about the case to the applicant.

4 Consider using professional representation in contestable cases rather than representing yourself, especially if time is important to you. If you nominate a representative, all further correspondence from the tribunal will be sent to them. Ensure your representative keeps you informed of developments.

5 In redundancy cases, if financial difficulties prevent you paying the applicant, mention this on your notice of appearance. Always pay promptly when a tribunal makes an award against you.

6 Prepare thoroughly for the hearing. Bring any documents that may be required as evidence. The tribunal may consider broader aspects of the case than just those covered by the application. Be ready to answer such questions. Ask the chairperson for advice if you need it; s/he is there to guide proceedings.

7 Postponement or adjournment due to failure to provide reasonable evidence (eg, about the continuing availability of an applicant's previous job) may make you liable for the costs incurred for additional hearings

Chapter 14 FOURTEEN

Getting payment from your customers

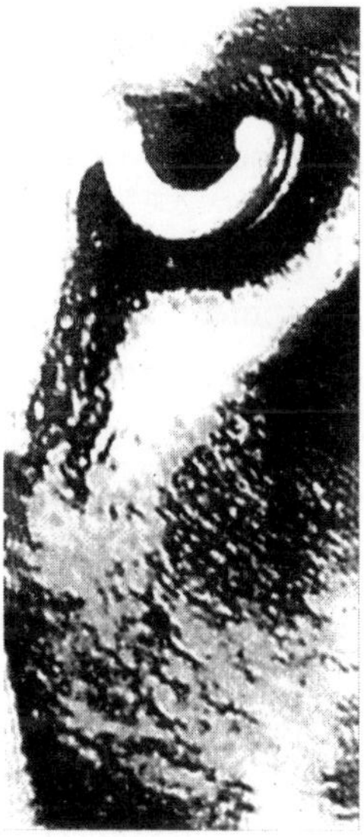

It is essential that you have firm control of your business finances. This chapter looks at negotiating payment from debtors.

Introduction

Companies without cash cannot survive. A company with thousands – or hundreds of thousands – of pounds worth of assets and a full order book can still go bust due to lack of cash with which to fund the business. A major contributory factor to the liquidity of a company is just how quickly you can get people to pay you.

This process begins with the negotiation of credit terms with your customers. You might offer standard terms of 30 days but have a customer who requires 60 days. How can you resolve the difference? If this is something that you do not want to live with – that is, you don't want to lose the customer but you do want your terms to be adhered to – how can you persuade him to pay you more swiftly than he pays others? If you are faced with such a situation, remember the golden rule – trade things that are inexpensive for you to provide, but valuable to the other party.

The primary objective of credit management is to turn debtors swiftly into cash, but without upsetting the business relationship. This requires careful handling. It is a balancing act between the necessity to impress upon the customer the need for and benefits of prompt payment, without being so heavy handed that you put them off dealing with you ever again; dealing with the present problem whilst keeping an eye on future opportunities.

The stages through which a customer may move whilst dealing with your company are as follows.

Credit checking

The initial decision as to whether you should accept the customer, leading to the setting of credit limits and the agreement of credit terms; it is particularly important that a small business should consider likely payment times before accepting a contract, particularly one from a larger company, which can take months to pay irrespective of terms.

Cash collection

This is the action taken when an account becomes overdue, generally consisting of reminder letters and cash collection calls.

Debt recovery

This is the action taken when cash collection does not work, it often involves legal action.

This chapter concentrates on 'cash collection', as outlined above.

Credit control

When controlling your receivables ledger, it helps to have an established policy that lets both you and your customers know where they stand. The first step is to establish credit terms – net 14 or 30 days, for example, so that you know when collection action should commence. The two most commonly used methods are reminder letter and/or telephone collection.

Reminder letters

Reminder letters must go out when the account becomes overdue; say at around 40 days for a 30 day account, to give the stragglers a chance to get their payments in. It is not worth having a series of reminders, as people will get to know the sequence and wait for the last one before taking action. Have one, and make sure it is specific and to the point.

Often letters have a sentence stating that you should ignore the letter if payment has already been made. Rather than doing that, ask people who have made payment to get in touch with the details immediately – after all, you do not want to give people the impression that it is okay to ignore your correspondence.

Reminder letters are one-way communication and should not ideally be the only collection method used. They are much more effective if followed up by a telephone collection call, which allows you the opportunity to gather information and to negotiate a way forward.

Telephone collection calls

Before you pick up the phone to make a tele-collection call, there are a number of things you should do. It is essential that you prepare thoroughly, and that you are as prepared as possible for the kinds of excuses for non-payment that you might be faced with. Whilst it may not be possible to be prepared for every eventuality, by making sure that you are informed and aware, you should be able to cope with the majority of situations.

Pre-call preparation

Before you pick up the phone to make a call, there are some things you should know:

- How do things stand? Exactly how much exactly does your customer owe? How old is the debt? Have any queries been raised? If so, have they been satisfactorily resolved?
- What has happened in the past? How have they paid previously? Have they always paid late, but have you just noticed the fact? Is their late payment this time a deviation from the norm? Is this an established customer?
- To whom do you need to speak? You need the name of the person who can authorise payment. If necessary, make a separate call to be sure the information you have is correct.
- What do you want to achieve? What will make it worth your while to pick up the phone? Set primary and secondary objectives. Your primary objective will generally be to negotiate payment of the account, in full, immediately. Your secondary objective will depend on the circumstances, but may be to negotiate payment of all but the current and/or any queried amount. Consider also your BATNA – your Best Alternative To a Negotiated Agreement – if you cannot achieve either your primary or secondary objectives, what would be your best alternative?

Making the call

When you are put through to your contact, you should:

- Introduce yourself by name.
- Listen actively, and let the customer know that you are listening.
- Question effectively, to gain information and keep control. A good opening question to use is 'Is there any reason why this account cannot be paid in full today?' It requires a yes or no answer only; if the answer is yes, you can then go on to get more information, if the answer is no, the customer has no reason not to agree to make payment. (If you opened with, for example, 'Why is it that you haven't paid?' then you are inviting an excuse – we need a copy invoice, this is in query, or whatever.)
- Use silence to bring pressure to bear. After someone has been asked a difficult question, they may need thinking time; alternatively, they could be on the hook. If you open with the suggested question, then it is essential that you remain silent afterwards and allow the customer time to reply. If you break the silence and ask, for example, 'Did you get the invoice?' then you are making the customer's excuses for him! Don't! Give him a little thinking time and allow the silence to pressure him.
- Get a commitment to pay from the customer. After all, that's the entire point of the call. If you end without getting promise of payment by a particular date then you are guilty of the same error committed by the salesman who ends his sales interview without asking for the order.

Further action

Taking further action (legal action, for example) can be expensive and also costs you the customer. However, there are some habitual debtors who only ever pay on receipt of a court summons, and in such cases the appropriate action should be taken. Purchasing sanctions are often more effective when they are at the back of the customer's mind rather than being used. If sanctions are taken then the customer has an excuse to stop talking with you, and it is generally easy enough to open up a line of credit elsewhere. Beware of bluffing – once you have made a threat, you must either follow it through or else lose credibility in the eyes of the customer.

Follow-up action

You should always keep full call detail records, which should include:

- the date and time of the call;
- to whom it was that you spoke;
- the main points of the conversation; and,
- when you should receive payment.

It goes without saying that you should always do what you said you would do, when you said you would do it. If you said you would resolve a problem by Wednesday, then make sure you do; if you said you would ring after seven days if no cheque was received, then make sure that you make that call.

Payment delay tactics

Some of the more common excuses offered by debtors for non-payment and some suggested responses are detailed below.

The cheque needs a second signature

This is a genuine requirement of some companies, but is used by many others as a delaying tactic. You can check if it's genuine or not by asking to speak to the signatory – if it is genuine, you will be put through and can plead the urgency of the case first hand, if it is not, then your request will be refused and you will have to question further to find the real reason.

We'll look into it and ring you back

Bet they don't! Always be in charge of calls – use your initiative and offer to ring the customer back at a pre-arranged time, or else say 'If you don't call me, I'll be sure to ring you.' That way, they know that you mean business.

The cheque is in the post

Possibly it is, but it's more likely that it isn't. Ask for details – cheque number, amount, date sent, whether it was first or second class, if it was marked for anyone's attention and so on. If it is in the post, then you'll get the information. If it isn't, you should get your cheque promptly and – as a bonus – the excuse probably won't be offered again. If no cheque arrives, call again within days, rather than weeks.

Your invoice is in the computer for payment

If you are prepared to live with this, fine. If you aren't, ask for a manually raised cheque. All companies can do this, although some are less willing than others.

The person you wish to speak to is not available

This could be genuine, but if you find it is happening regularly and you believe you are being stalled, escalate the call. Ask for the managing director or the financial director – no one is too important for you to speak to, and taking this approach shows that you mean business.

That invoice is in query

Ask for full details of the query, the name of the person dealing with it, and payment of the undisputed amount. If the customer digs his heels in, check out the query and see that it is resolved as speedily as possible. Once all obstacles to payment have been removed, you should get your cheque.

Could you send a copy invoice?

A simple and commonly used tactic, and yet one which can prove difficult to handle. If they insist copies are necessary, fax them if possible; write on the invoices 'This is a bona fide copy invoice', sign it and date it. That way if your customer then tries to insist that a fax is not a legal document, you are covered. If you have a customer who habitually asks for copies, consider charging for them; it's not unreasonable, and if this is just a delaying tactic then it will stop. Alternatively, send the copies as a matter of course before making the call; that way you effectively remove the reason for non-payment.

Our payment conditions are...

Faced with this one, check the documentation just in case something was written in; at the end of the day, supplier's terms take precedence anyway, but being sure of your facts will stand you in better stead to negotiate. Check out the customer's payment terms and try to be included on their prompt payment list.

The person who signs the cheques is away from the office

This is often used as an excuse and delaying tactic. Try to determine how long the absence is for and find out if anyone else can sign cheques (speak to them if there is someone). Press for a promise of settlement with a set date for action and call back if nothing is forthcoming (or call back at 9.00 am on the first day the signatory is back in the office, to stress the urgency of the situation). Ultimately it is illegal for a company to continue to trade when they cannot carry out their business properly; consider asking to speak to a director if you are getting nowhere fast.

We are changing banks

This can cause delays but is normally quite straightforward. Confirm the balance outstanding and take details of the new bank – suggest they apply for an emergency chequebook, if they don't have one already, or suggest that they use another method of payment; there is no reason why changing banks should stop payments being made.

We are going through a re-organisation (or take-over)

Take an interest and show concern, that way you'll get more information about what's going on. Offer to call (or to have a sales person call) when the changes are complete – and go for full settlement; they should be able at least to raise a manual cheque.

Do you want my business or not?

This is a particularly nasty form of blackmail, especially when used against a small business by a larger concern. The best way to deal with this sort of comment is not to rise to the bait but to say, 'Of course we want your business, Mr Smith, you are a valued customer; but payment of the account within the terms agreed is all part of a business transaction. Extended credit has to be paid for by someone and it would be a shame to see it reflected in the customer tariff. Prompt payment enables customers to benefit from competitive prices and this would be affected if customers were to take unofficial extended credit.'

We can't really say when it will be paid

If the customer is completely evasive then it is up to you to try to establish the real reason for non-payment. If the problem is a shortage of cash, then that is not just the customer's problem, it is your problem too. Make that clear and then move on to see how you can work together to sort things out and find a solution. If you decide to go for timed instalments, be specific about amounts and due dates. Be sure to monitor the situation and keep track of your customer's financial position.

The cheque is received but with no signature

Make a call to acknowledge receipt of the cheque and bear in mind that it could have been an oversight, but press hard for agreement on the date of receipt of the signed or replacement cheque.

Conclusion

Getting payment of an account is all part of the business relationship. Good communication skills are essential, as are good negotiating skills. You need to know what you want to achieve and also to know your BATNA. If you cannot negotiate payment in full, or of all but the current and queried debt, then your BATNA might be return of the goods supplied, if appropriate, or some form of agreed instalments to clear off the debt, plus prepayment of any orders placed in the meantime. Remember to take the long-term view – your customer might be in difficulties now, but this problem may be only short-term.

Useful **tips**

1. Prepare thoroughly and set objectives before contacting a customer.

2. Be prepared for standard excuses and have a method of dealing with them.

3. Question for further information and propose what you believe to be an acceptable course of action

4. Do not allow the customer to fob you off – deal with factual information and negotiate a commitment to pay.
5. Remember to be assertive at all times.

Part 4FOUR

Appendices

Chapter 15 FIFTEEN

Further reading

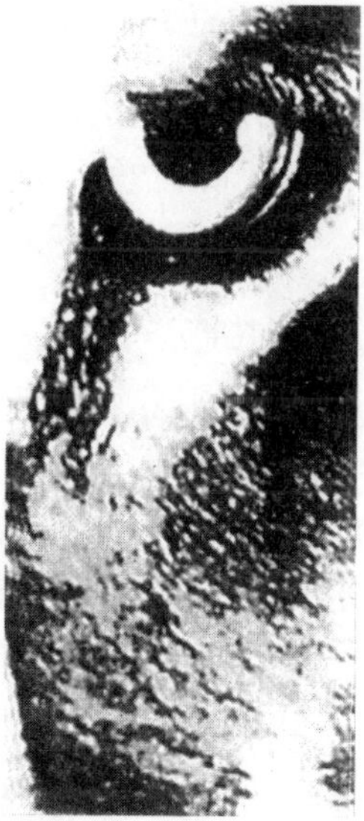

Chapter 1

Effective Negotiating, Colin Robinson, Kogan Page, 1996.

The Language of Negotiation, Joan Mulholland, Routledge, 1991.

Successful Negotiating, Peter Fleming, Barrons, 1997.

Negotiating: Everybody Wins, Vanessa Helps, BBC Publications, 1992.

How to be a Better Negotiator, John Mattock and Jons Ehrenborg, Kogan Page, 1996.

Chapter 2

Effective Negotiating, Colin Robinson, Kogan Page, 1996.

The Language of Negotiation, Joan Mulholland, Routledge, 1991.

Successful Negotiating, Peter Fleming, Barrons, 1997.

Negotiating: Everybody Wins, Vanessa Helps, BBC Publications, 1992.

How to be a Better Negotiator, John Mattock and Jons Ehrenborg, Kogan Page, 1996.

Mastering Negotiations, Eric Evans, Hawksmere, 1998.

Chapter 3

How to be a Better Negotiator, John Mattock and Jons Ehrenborg, Kogan Page, 1996.

Serious Creativity, Dr Edward de Bono, HarperCollins Publishers, 1992.

Chapter 4

Managing Stress: Emotion and Power at Work, Tim Newton, Sage, 1995.

Help Yourself to Better Health: Managing Pressure, BUPA, 1996.

Managing Stress: Keeping Calm Under Fire, Barbara Braham, Irwin, 1994.

Pressure at Work, T Arroba & K James, McGraw Hill, 1992.

The Book of Stress Survival, Alix Kirsta, Thorsons, 1992.

Chapter 5

Power – Creating it, Using it, Helga Drummond, Kogan Page, 1992.

Chapter 6

How to be a Better Negotiator, John Mattock and Jons Ehrenborg, Kogan Page, 1996.

Negotiating: Everybody Wins, Vanessa Helps, BBC Publications, 1992.

Chapter 7

How to be a Better Negotiator, John Mattock and Jons Ehrenborg, Kogan Page, 1996.

Managing Cultural Diversity at Work, June Jackson and Khizar Humayun Ansari, Kogan Page, 1995.

Chapter 8

Ask the Right Question, Rupert Eales-White, McGraw Hill, 1997.

Getting Value from Professional Advisers, Catriona Standish, Kogan Page, 1993.

How to Select and Use Consultants, Milan Kubr, International Labour Office, 1993.

Chapter 9

Getting to Yes, Roger Fisher and William Ury, Hutchinson, 1990.

Handling Conflict and Negotiation, Manchester Open Learning, Kogan Page, 1995.

Chapter 10

Assertiveness at Work, Kate and Ken Back, McGraw-Hill, 1992.

Putting Assertiveness to Work: A Programme for Management Excellence, Graham Willcocks and Steve Morris, Pitman Publishing, 1996.

Chapter 11

Tendering for Government Contracts, and *Business in Europe*, Department of Trade and Industry Publications Order Line: (0870) 150 2500.

Contrax Weekly, Business Information Publications Ltd, Tel: (0141) 332 8247.

Supplement S, Tenders Electronic Daily (TED), and *Official Journal of the European Communities*, HMSO, Tel: (0207) 873 9090 (Individual copies), Tel: (0207) 873 8409 (Subscriptions).

Europa – European Union Server, Website: www.europa.eu.int.

For information on tendering in Europe contact your local Euro-Information Centre. Details of your nearest EIC are available from the European Commission London Office. Tel: (0207) 973 1992.

The UK Network of Euro-Information Centres has a national web site: www.euro-info.org.uk.

For information and advice on obtaining a quality assurance certificate contact your local Training and Enterprise Council (TEC) or the Institute of Quality Assurance (see below):

Tendering for MOD Contracts, Tim Boyce, Hawksmere, 1998.

Negotiating with the MOD, Tim Boyce, Hawksmere, 1997.

Chapter 12

Employee Relations, R Bennett, Pitman Publishing, 1997.

Butterworth's Employment Law Guide,
Butterworth Heinemann, 1996.

Labour Law: Management Decisions and Workers Rights,
S Anderman, Butterworth Heinemann, 1993.

Trade Unions, Employers and the Law, G Morris and T J Archer,
Butterworth Heinemann, 1993.

Employment Relations, Hartley and Stephenson (editors), Blackwell, 1992.

Trade Unions and Labour Relations (Consolidation) Act 1992, available from HMSO bookshops.

Trade Union Reform and Employment Rights Act 1993, available from HMSO bookshops.

Chapter 13

The following booklets are available from your local employment service and the Employment Tribunals Service. Separate booklets are available to cover Scotland.

Understanding Industrial Tribunals – What do Industrial Tribunals do? Employment Tribunals Service (ITL booklet 1).

Understanding Industrial Tribunals – How to apply to an Industrial Tribunal, Employment Tribunals Service (ITL booklet 2).

Understanding Industrial Tribunals – What to do if taken to an Industrial Tribunal, Employment Tribunals Service (ITL booklet 3).

Understanding Industrial Tribunals – Hearings at Industrial Tribunals, Employment Tribunals Service (ITL booklet 4).

Chapter 14

The Credit Controllers Desktop Guide, Roger Mason, Hawksmere, 1999.

The Credit Management Handbook, Edited by Burt Edwards, Gower, 1990.

How to get Debts Paid Faster, Roy Hedges, Gower, 1990.

Financial Control for Non-Financial Managers, David Irwin, Pitman Publishing, 1995.

Chapter 16SIXTEEN

Useful addresses

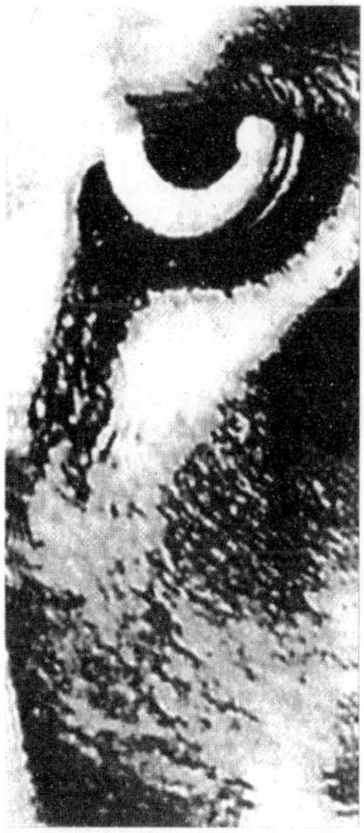

Addresses and telephone numbers for your local Business Link, Training and Enterprise Council (TEC) (Local Enterprise Company (LEC) in Scotland) and Local Enterprise Agency may be found in your telephone directory. Your local TEC or LEC will be able to provide information about training in negotiating skills.

The Business Link Signpost service on (0345) 567 765 can put you in touch with your nearest Business Link office. Local Scottish Business Shops can be contacted on (0141) 248 6014 or (0800) 787 878 for callers from Scotland. For Business Connect in Wales call (0345) 969 798. The Local Enterprise Development Unit (LEDU) in Northern Ireland can be contacted on (01232) 491 031.

The National Federation of Enterprise Agencies can put you in touch with your nearest agency. Ring them on 01234 354055 or look on the Internet at http://www.nfea.com

Shell *Live*WIRE helps young people to explore the option of starting or developing their own business. Ring them on (0191) 261 5584 or look on the Internet at http://www/shell-livewire.org

Project North East, through its subsidiary, Cobweb Information Ltd, publishes *Business Information Factsheets (BIF)*, which each give an overview of a different aspect of business, with signposts to further information. To date over 350 factsheets have been published. BIFs are available from Business Links, enterprise agencies and libraries. If you have difficulty finding BIFs locally, contact PNE directly. PNE also publishes *Market Synopses*: concise but comprehensive reports covering major UK market sectors. Synopses can be purchased individually directly from PNE:

Hawthorn House, Forth Banks, Newcastle upon Tyne, NE1 3SG.
Tel: 0191 261 7856 • Fax: 0191 261 1910
e-mail: cobweb@projectne.co.uk

Project North East has set up an Internet site which may be of interest to anyone starting or already in business at http://www.pne.org/cobweb

Advisory, Conciliation and Arbitration Service (ACAS)
Brandon House
180 Borough High Street
London SE1 1LW
Tel: (0207) 210 3000

The address of your local ACAS office is in the telephone book.

Certification Officer for Trade Unions and Employers' Associations
Brandon House
180 Borough High Street
London SE1 1LW
Tel: (0207) 210 3735

Employment Tribunals Service
Enquiry Line: (0345) 959 775
(covers England, Wales and Scotland)

Irish Congress of Trade Unions
19 Raglan Road
Ballsbridge
Dublin 4
Ireland
Tel: (+353) 1 668 0641
Website: www.iol.ie/ictu/

Northern Ireland Committee
Irish Congress of Trade Unions
3 Wellington Park
Belfast BT9 6DJ
Northern Ireland
Tel: (01232) 681 726
Website: www.iol.ie/ictu/

Office of Fair Trading
Unfair Contract Terms Unit
Room 505, Field House
15-25 Beam Buildings
London EC4A 1PR
Tel: (0207) 211 8000

Scottish Trade Union Congress
333 Woodlands Road
Glasgow
Scotland G3 6NG
Tel: (0141) 337 8100

Trade Union Congress (TUC)
Congress House
23-28 Great Russell Street
London WC1B 3LS
Tel: (0207) 636 4030
Website: www.tuc.org.uk

Index

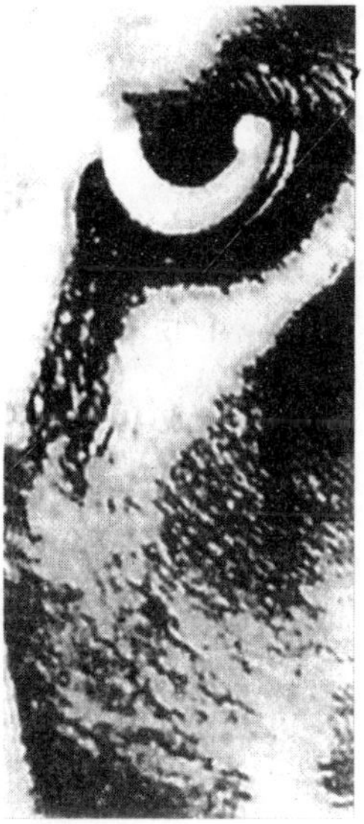